THE GREAT EXTRAVAGANZA

The Great Extravaganza: Portland and the Lewis and Clark Exposition tells the story of a great event a century ago. This 1905 world's fair commemorated the diplomatic quest for knowledge and scientific information that President Thomas Jefferson sent west with Lewis and Clark and their "Corps of Discovery" during their 1803-06 expedition. It also introduced Portland, Oregon to the world and was a catalyst for boosterism and development in the state at large.

In 2005, the Pacific Northwest will bring visitors from afar to rediscover our land and waters, and Oregon will invoke the great mind of our third president, bringing together the world's greatest artists and thinkers to reflect on the preceding centuries and the century dawning before us. Our region will play a leading role in commemorating the national bicentennial of the Lewis and Clark Expedition. Now, as we reissue this popular history of the 1905 Lewis and Clark Centennial Exposition and Oriental Fair, let us begin to write a new episode of Lewis and Clark for the next century!

Chet Orloff
Executive Director
Oregon Historical Society

Unlike so many other large-scale fairs and expositions, the 1905 Lewis and Clark Centennial and American Pacific Exposition and Oriental Fair in Portland, Oregon was a success, especially historically and financially. The economic impact of the audaciously planned fair on the northern outskirts of Portland is with us still. The astute and bold planning of so long ago continues to produce handsomely for the entire Oregon community.

I have long had a keen interest in the Lewis and Clark Exposition, and one of my favorite personal collections is built of objects associated with our greatest Oregon fair. It is a historical, sentimental, family-related interest that has afforded me many pleasant hours, for my own family's business started with an exhibit that my father installed most successfully in that memorable summer of 1905. So it is with genuine personal pleasure that I recommend this long-awaited study.

Victor G. Atiyeh
Governor, 1979-1987
The State of Oregon

OPENED
JUNE 1ST
1905
CLOSES
OCT. 15TH

THE GREAT EXTRAVAGANZA

Portland and the Lewis and Clark Exposition

CARL ABBOTT

Oregon Historical Society

Dedicated to the memory of
LEWIS BERKELEY COX
As a Board Director of the
OREGON HISTORICAL SOCIETY
it was his idea that the Portland Exposition
commemorate the centennial of the
Lewis and Clark Expedition

The Oregon Historical Society would like to thank
the LORENE SAILS HIGGINS CHARITABLE TRUST
for their support of this new edition.

Cover: Bird's eye view of the Lewis & Clark Exposition
Back cover: Night time view of the Fair

Printed in the United States of America

Rev. edition 1996
For more information on Oregon Historical Society publications, try www.ohs.org, orhist@ohs.org, or write to us at Oregon Historical Society Press, 1200 SW Park, Portland, Oregon 97205-2483

Library of Congress Catalog Card Number 80-83179

Library of Congress Cataloging in Publication Data
Abbott, Carl.
The Great Extravaganza.
Bibliography: p.
Includes index.
1. Lewis and Clark Centennial Exposition (1905: Portland, Or.) I. Title.
T834.B1A2 973.91'1'0074019549 80-83179
ISBN 0-87595-088-4 AACR2

Contents

Illustrations

Illustrations with OrHi reference are from the Oregon Historical Society Photographic Archive

THE GREAT EXTRAVAGANZA

Flag flown over the Exposition on Opening Day, 1 June, 1905.

I

June 1, 1905

By the end of the opening ceremonies, Portland's business leaders could breathe with relief. Little things had gone wrong for the first day of the Lewis and Clark Exposition, but the big things had gone right.

The final touch at 10:00 P.M. was a cascade of fireworks from barges moored in Guild's Lake. Puffing their well-earned cigars, J.C. Ainsworth, Henry Ladd Corbett, Henry W. Goode and the other representatives of the Exposition watched from the terrace behind the Agriculture Building. For the last three hours they had bent elbows with Vice President Charles Fairbanks and U.S. House Speaker Joe Cannon at the formal banquet. Now they stood shoulder-to-shoulder with the city's national guests and welcomed the cool air off the Willamette after their long days of worry over last-minute details.

Invitations to the festivities had been part of the publicity campaign. The "List of Distinguished Persons to be Invited to the Formal Opening of the Lewis and Clark Exposition" ran to 1,877 names, starting with Lyman Abbott, editor of the high-minded Brooklyn, New York-based *Outlook*, and ending with Eugene Zimmerman, president of the Cincinnati, Hamilton and Dayton Railroad. The organizers were scarcely bothered by the shower of polite refusals, for their main concern was to impress the official federal delegation that had arrived at 9:00 P.M. on May 31. Though this party was an hour late because of delays in Seattle, the band had still been ready with the vice-presidential march and the champagne had still been kept cold at the Portland Hotel. Most of the party had retired before midnight to suites in the hotel after shaking the important hands of Portland. Charles Fairbanks and his family enjoyed an extra drive across the city to spend the night at the home of Exposition President Henry Goode on the southwest corner of Twentieth and Flanders.

June 1 was a perfect Portland day for the end of spring. Winds from the south and southwest had carried bands of clouds and rain in the early morning, but the sky cleared and the temperature climbed to the upper sixties by noon. The leading detachments of the parade marshaled at Sixth and Montgomery, with a contingent of mounted police followed by the band and first squadron of the Fourth U.S. Cavalry. Other elements formed up on the residential side streets of Mill, Market, and Clay and stepped into place as the parade marched along Sixth Street—the Fourteenth U.S. Infantry, 2,000 members of the National Guard, and more police to bring up the rear. At 10:30, in front of the Portland Hotel, the ranks opened for the carriages of vice president, congressmen, visiting governors, and other dignitaries to swing out of the hotel's circular drive and into line behind the cavalry.

The best views were from the upper floors of the Oregonian Building where idle copyboys watched the parade turn from Sixth west onto Alder. To their right, through the thick crowd, the visitors could glimpse the window-shopping blocks that stretched to Third Street between Alder and Washington. Up the hill behind them, the Court House and the Portland Hotel marked the division between the residential and commercial sections. Further south were occasional mansions surrounded by block after block of small frame houses and tenements. To the north was the growing business district, where older office blocks on Third and Fourth were suffering from the competition of newer six- and eight-story buildings.

Tourists who caught the parade downtown could find more than enough entertainment without fighting for a place on the streetcars to the Exposition grounds. The three big department stores had declared a holiday for June 1, but there was no problem in buying a nickel glass of Henry Weinhard's beer and taking a leisurely lunch until the theatres opened. The Belasco Theatre was directly on the parade route at Fourteenth and Washington. Tickets ranged from 15¢ to 75¢ for its matinee performance of the popular drama "The Heart of Maryland." The dime theatres offered melodrama and variety acts. Under the management of future mayor George L. Baker, the Empire was unveiling "A Wicked Woman." The Star, at Park and Washington, listed a full card of vaudeville. General admission was a dime but front-row seats for the evening performances sold for half a dollar.

The crowds on the sidewalks thinned as the parade zigzagged across the third and second wards—Alder to Fourteenth to Everett to Twentieth to Overton to Twenty-Fourth to Savier and finally to Twenty-Eighth. The route carefully avoided Chinatown at the foot of Burnside, where 1,000 Japanese and 7,000 Chinese lived clustered in a few blocks near the river. Instead, the route gave the guests a glimpse of the workingclass city.

The long slope of northwest Portland between the Northern Pacific rail yards and the grand homes at the base of the hills housed 25,000 people. Two-thirds of them rented their apartments and cottages. One-fifth had been born in Europe and another fifth were children of immigrants. By indicators in the census, there was little to differentiate them from the 20,000 residents of south Portland where the parade had started. There were more Italians and Jews south of the business core and more Germans, Swedes, and Slavs to the north, but both neighborhoods provided the muscle power for Portland wharves and factories.

The opening day attendance at the Exposition itself fell just below 40,000, considerably short of the projected 75,000. By mid-morning impatient crowds broke their lines to push and clamor around the ticket booths. There was jostling and shoving but no serious disorder as the clerks grabbed for the dimes and quarters. Inside the gates, the visitors found an Exposition that the management had declared to be precisely ninety-seven percent complete. A few piles of crates and lumber littered the back corners of the grounds, but the exhibition buildings and their formal plazas were ready for business. Only one or two storefronts were empty in the amusement row along "The Trail." The cones were stacked at the ice cream stands, the postcards were racked, the sausages were steaming, and the pride of Portland was on display.

When the cavalry band led the mile-long procession through the Twenty-Eighth Street carriage entrance, fairgoers began to drift toward the Lake View Terrace and the speakers' platform. A round of applause greeted the guests who filed out of the New York Building a few minutes before noon. The audience cheered again for the welcome by Henry Goode and settled in for a siege of speechmaking as Goode launched into an endorsement of the "resistless progress" of the Pacific Coast. For an hour-and-a-half, one speaker after another repeated the tribute: Governor George Earle Chamberlain, president of the Lewis and Clark Centennial Exposition Commission Jefferson Myers, Mayor George H. Williams, Senator C.D. Clark of Wyoming, Congressman J.A. Tawney of Minnesota, Assistant Treasury Secretary H.A. Taylor from the federal Lewis and Clark Exposition Board—these men of substance and position agreed that Portland had provided a regional celebration of national importance.

The speakers took their theme from the motto over the entrance to the Exposition—"Westward The Course Of Empire Takes Its Way." Their concern was the Fair's ability to call public attention to the development of California, Oregon, and Washington. Behind the rhetoric was the assumption that the twentieth century was to be America's Pacific century. The nation was firmly established around the Pacific rim in Panama, Alaska, Hawaii and the Philippines, with stepping stones at Samoa and Guam. The "final and definitive" policy of the Open Door to China promised the realization of the old American dream of the oriental market. As Goode had put it the year before, the first large international exposition on the West Coast would "demonstrate to the commercial world . . . the actual inception of the era of new trade relations with the teeming millions of Asiatic countries."

The eighth speech (not counting the invocation) was by "Uncle Joe" Cannon of Missouri. He had barely acknowledged the wave of shouts and cheers when Henry Goode stepped forward to announce that a telegram had just informed President Theodore Roosevelt that the Exposition was ready for business. The President responded at 1:22 P.M. by thumping a golden telegraph key in the East Room of the White House to trigger the chimes in the twin towers of the U.S. Govern-

A view northeast across the fringe of Portland's downtown residential area to the Willamette and the city's riverfront industrial area. Guild's Lake appears to the left. Across the Willamette lies Portland's relatively undeveloped northeast side, with the Columbia River visible beyond; Washington state, on the far side of the Columbia, forms the horizon. The scenes on this and the opposite page are part of a 1903 photographic panorama, taken from the city's west hills.

This view looks east across the heart of downtown Portland. The intersection of Sixth and Yamhill (pictured on page 8) is to the right of the Meier & Frank building (center right), home of the city's leading department store. The Willamette River, separating Portland's downtown from the city's east side, cuts horizontally through this vista. The largest building in the foreground is the Portland Exposition Building, first used in 1889.

President Roosevelt's personal emissary as well as the federal government's appointed representative, Vice President Charles Fairbanks highlighted the Exposition's VIP guest list for the opening ceremonies. In this photograph (ABOVE) of the official party on opening day, Fairbanks stands out as the tallest figure; Exposition president H.W. Goode appears at his right.

In 1900, Portland's west side housed about twice as many residents as those living across the river. This 1908 map of Portland (RIGHT) indicates the rapid eastside development that took place in the years following the Lewis and Clark Exposition. In 1910, at the height of the building boom, 3,000 houses were constructed east of the Willamette, compared to only 132 on the west side.

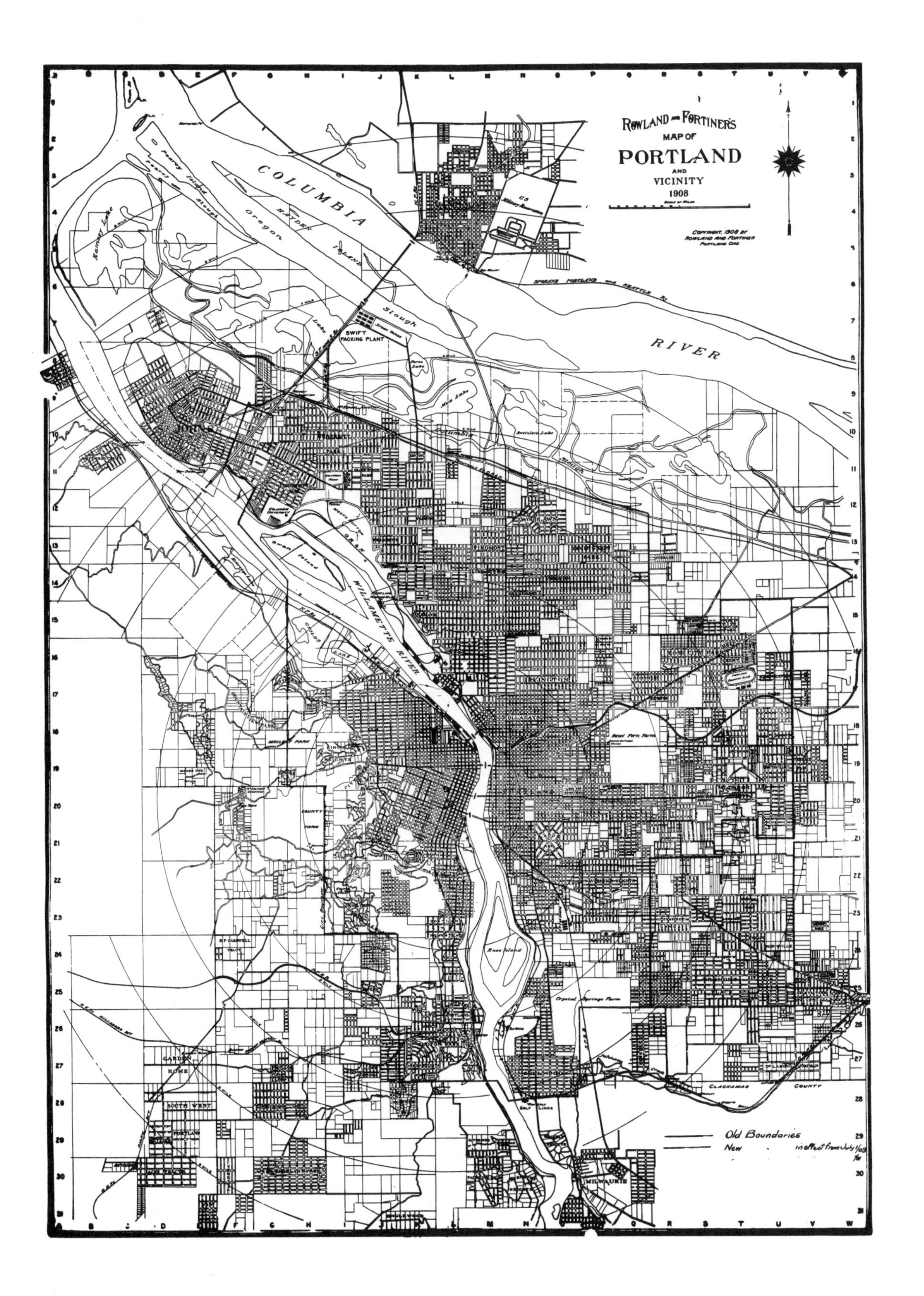
ROWLAND AND FORTINER'S
MAP OF
PORTLAND
AND
VICINITY
1908
COPYRIGHT, 1908 BY
ROWLAND AND FORTINER
PORTLAND ORE.
COLUMBIA
RIVER
SWIFT PACKING PLANT
WILLAMETTE RIVER
CLACKAMAS
COUNTY
MILWAUKIE
Old Boundaries
New
in effect from July 1/08

Along with pride about its position of West Coast commercial importance, Portland considered itself a worthy rival, culturally and aesthetically, of its refined older sisters on the East Coast. The city was proud of its tree-lined, paved and lighted streets, its distinguished hotels, its architecture and its efficient transportation. This view from Taylor Street of turn-of-the-century downtown looks north along Sixth Avenue. The three large buildings on the left-hand side are the Portland Hotel, Marquam Building (in 1905 it housed offices and a theater; the edifice collapsed in 1912) and the Oregonian Building, headquarters for the state's largest newspaper.

At the turn of the century, publicity about Portland invariably included a photograph of the busy Willamette River, the city's harbor, for this was the symbol of Portland's—and the state's—commercial prosperity and potential growth. Here, at the "Gateway to the Pacific Northwest," boat- and train-loads of lumber, grain and other agricultural products brought from the interior were loaded onto ocean-going ships bound for foreign markets.

ment Building. Somewhere along the 3,000 miles was a gap in the circuit. The crowd waited expectantly for a minute, and for another, and then for another, until Goode stepped forward again with a second telegram to report that Roosevelt had done his job and that the Fair was officially open. Joe Cannon shouted the restless audience into silence and proceeded with the longest speech of the afternoon, with further interruptions when the Innes Band struck up "America" and "The Star-Spangled Banner."

Charles Fairbanks had the honor of the last address. While the crowd shifted and shuffled, he invoked the spirit of Thomas Jefferson, praised William Clark and Meriwether Lewis, and quoted the martyred McKinley's statement that "expositions are the timekeepers of progress." Like the other speakers, he carefully noted the expansion of American power in the Pacific and praised the cities, farms, industries and railroads of the Great Northwest. He finished with the touch of a politician playing to his audience:

There is no seer with vision so penetrating that he can forecast the future possibilities of this people in all of the manifold avenues of human efforts. Who would attempt to mirror the developments upon the West Coast one hundred years hence? . . . Yes, who will venture to foretell the measure of your upbuilding in the quarter of a century beyond the present hour?

The Exposition was not the only entertainment in the northwest end of Portland. Many in the overflow crowd trickled away from the oratory to stroll three blocks to the Pacific Coast League baseball park at Twenty-Fourth and Vaughn, where the Portland Giants were staging a six-game home stand against the Seattle Indians. Four thousand fans enjoyed the afternoon sunshine and watched the Giants raise their record to 26–27 and a tie for fourth place. As a local sportswriter recounted the contest, the "Siwashes" hit Portland for seven "bingles," two of them for "extra cushions," but the Seattle nine could push only two runs across the plate. The Giants came back to "cut five notches" in the "sixth stanza." They had the help of confusion in the Seattle outfield, a nonchalant umpire, and a bad throw that sailed over the outstretched glove of the firstbagger to land among the 25¢ patrons sitting in the "land of bleach."

Like the fans who cheered for Portland baseball against the rivalry of Seattle, Tacoma, San Francisco, Oakland, and Los Angeles, Portland businessmen also lived in a world of urban competition. It was scarcely polite to talk too openly in front of out-of-towners or to mar the opening ceremonies with economic details, but Portland's civic leaders expected the Exposition to reconfirm their city as the commercial capital of the Northwest. In their booster vision, they also saw the next step as dominance on the Pacific Coast. Puget Sound cities, after all, were still upstarts. Los Angeles was not even a seaport. San Francisco had seen better days. The Portland boosters' self-confidence was epitomized by an article by Harvey Scott in Portland's *Pacific Monthly* for July, 1905, entitled "The Momentous Struggle for Mastery of the Pacific." The subject was supposedly geopolitics, and the illustrations were all views of Portland and its Exposition.

In practical terms, said Henry Goode, the Exposition could advertise Portland and secure new immigrants for the West's wealthiest, most attractive, and most progressive city. It could help to triple Oregon's population, said Jefferson Myers. New settlers would mean more lumber and grain to be loaded for China and Japan at Portland docks, for steam and electricity had established "neighborhood relations" between the western states and the Orient. Although other ports were contending for the same business, the *Oregonian* echoed an old Portland conviction when it argued that the metropolis of the Columbia controlled the natural routes of commerce. The conclusion was simple to those who could read the landscape: "Portland was chosen by a decree of fate which inertia, obstinacy or folly may postpone, but never alter."

In hope and in fact, the entrance to the Exposition grounds was also Portland's gateway to the twentieth century. Mayor Williams stated the theme on June 1 when he asserted that the Exposition "represents the great things of a wonder-working century." The extravaganza of a world's fair gave Portland a chance to show itself off and opened new opportunities for growth. It offered an older generation an occasion to work the strings of power one more time, and it gave a new generation the chance to shape the city in which it wanted to live. Before the Exposition was a month old, Portlanders were certain that it marked the beginning of a new era. Within a year, they agreed that it had divided the old Oregon from the new. For the seventy-five years since, the Lewis and Clark Exposition has remained in our memory as Portland's great community enterprise, the symbol of a hopeful era when the big things seemed to go right.

Officers and operations directors of the Lewis and Clark Centennial Exposition.

II

THE LEWIS AND CLARK CENTENNIAL EXPOSITION

A world's fair was a well-tested idea by the start of the twentieth century. In the press releases and speeches, industrial and scientific expositions were described as "schools of progress." For civic leaders in the club rooms and real estate offices, they were also international advertisements—great devices of salesmanship to attract investors and immigrants to their host city. The ostensible goal was often to commemorate a milestone in national history, but the impetus and organization came from the bankers, the boosters, and the boards of trade.

It was certainly businessmen who gave the idea to Portland. In the midst of a national depression in 1895, dry goods merchant Dan McAllen suggested that Portland mark the new century and pull itself out of its economic slump by holding some sort of international fair. Since Portland businessmen preferred to see any federal aid go to improving navigation at the bar of the Columbia, the idea attracted mild attention but no action. Four years later, the *Portland Evening Telegram* published a long article by Henry Dosch on a possible Oregon exposition. Dosch was a local manufacturer who had represented Oregon at the Columbian Exposition in Chicago in 1893 and at Omaha's Trans-Mississippi Exposition in 1898. Members of the National Editorial Association who met in Portland in July, 1899, endorsed the same idea of a 1902 fair for Oregon. Despite these endorsements the *Oregonian* scoffed at the suggestion, and the Portland Chamber of Commerce ignored it when Congressman Thomas Tongue of Hillsboro repeated the proposal in January, 1900.

Interest began to come together a few months later. J.M. Long of the Portland Board of Trade put together a provisional committee that met occasionally during the second half of 1900 to consider the possibilities of a Northwest industrial exposition. The date and theme came from the Oregon Historical Society. Meeting under the leadership of *Oregonian* editor Harvey Scott on December 15, 1900, the Society endorsed the suggestion for a commercial exposition to be held in conjunction with the centennial of Lewis and Clark's exploration of the Oregon Country. Two months later, the Oregon legislature endorsed the Historical Society's suggestion, pledged state aid once an effort was organized, and appointed five commissioners to report on progress to the next session; the chairman was Henry W. Corbett (president of the First National Bank, former United States senator, and undoubtedly the city's leading businessman), and the other members were Charles Bellinger of Portland, Henry Ankeny of Eugene, Charles Fulton of Astoria, and Edward Young of Baker.

A triumvirate of Corbett, Scott, and Long worked together through 1901 to transform the idea of a 1905 exposition into a businesslike proposition. During the spring, Long's provisional committee solicited support from the legislatures of Washington, Idaho, Montana, Utah, Colorado, and British Columbia. The state commission and the provisional committee of local business organizations jointly appointed a young *Oregonian* reporter, Henry Reed, their chief of publicity and tried to define realistic goals for a city of 100,000. The organizers filed articles of incorporation that had been prepared by J.M. Long on October 12. The name of the corporation, through which Portland's civic elite proposed to stage the fair summed up the dual goals of historic commemoration and regional boosterism: "The Lewis and Clark Centennial and American Pacific Exposition and Oriental Fair."

A mass meeting of Portland citizens on November 5, 1901, ratified the executive board that Henry Corbett had carefully picked to represent the solid business community. There were members from the Board of Trade, the Chamber of Commerce, the Manufacturers Association, and the incorporating committee and other members with the ability to supply voluntary legal and financial advice. Corbett himself chaired the corporation and pledged $30,000 when the stock subscription books were opened on November 25. The original $300,000 issue was oversubscribed within ten days. The Ladd and Tilton Bank took $20,000, the Northern Pacific Railroad another $20,000, and brewer Henry Weinhard $10,000. Approximately half the total came from twenty-nine pledges of $1,200 or more, but another 3,000 citizens shared in the financial commitment with subscriptions of $2.00 to $1,000.

The breakdown of stock purchases by companies and occupations shows the range of Portland businesses that hoped to benefit from an international exposition. A number of enterprises obviously expected to make money from an influx of tourists, with $12,000 pledged from hotels and restaurants, $20,000 from the streetcar companies, $20,000 from brewers and liquor dealers, and $40,000 from retailers. The steam railroads, which hoped to haul the visitors to Portland, invested $51,000. Most of the remainder came from businessmen ranging from land speculators to wholesalers to bankers, whose prosperity depended on the growth of Portland's commerce and population.

The decision to stage the Lewis and Clark Exposition put Portlanders into the mainstream of American boosterism. The permanent board of directors for the corporation, elected on January 13, 1902, perpetuated the business leadership of the previous year. As the board worked on plans for a comprehensive exposition that would remain within Portland's budget, they could draw on the experience of a dozen other cities. During the previous generation, the United States had held two world's fairs of truly national scope—the Centennial Exposition at Philadelphia in 1876 and the Columbian Exposition at Chicago in 1893. Other fairs had been geared to the needs and hopes of single cities, such as Atlanta's International Cotton Exposition in 1881 and its Piedmont Exposition in 1887, and the New Orleans Cotton Centennial Exposition in 1885. At the end of the century, expositions became a virtual mania, with the Nashville Centennial Exposition in 1897, the Trans-Mississippi Exposition at Omaha in 1898, and the Pan-American Exposition at Buffalo in 1901. Still to come were the Louisiana Purchase Exposition at St. Louis in 1904, the Lewis and Clark in 1905, the Jamestown Tercentennial in Norfolk in 1907, the Alaska-Yukon-Pacific in Seattle in 1909, and the Panama-Pacific in San Francisco in 1915.

In the middle of this exposition fad, the first job of the Lewis and Clark management was to convince state legislatures and congressional committees to share the costs of yet another fair on the distant West Coast. During 1903 the corporation dispatched five special agents to stalk the corridors of western capitols and cadge votes in the nearby barrooms. At the year's end, D.C. Freeman, C.H. McIsaac, and the other lobbyists reported success in Sacramento, Boise, Salt Lake, Helena, Bismarck, St. Paul, and Jefferson City. Sixteen states in total came through with appropriations for exhibits and ten would construct special buildings: Maine, Colorado, Idaho, Utah, and Illinois erected modest exhibit buildings; Missouri, Massachusetts and New York built larger structures to match their population and importance; and, with buildings that rivaled some of the main halls, Washington and California took advantage of the opportunity offered by the first western exposition.

Official participation by Oregon was a foregone conclusion. Portlanders were careful to point out that the Fair was designed to attract attention to the entire state for "the development of our material resources and manufacturing interests," and the legislature acted early in 1903 to appropriate $450,000 for an exhibition of Oregon's "arts, industries, manufactures, and products" to be held in Portland in 1905 in cooperation and conjunction with the work of the Lewis and Clark Exposition Company. To oversee the state effort, the legislators established a Lewis and Clark Centennial Exposition Commission, chaired by Jefferson Myers of Salem and including four members from Portland and five from downstate. The legislative judgment was clear that the corporation was to organize, promote, and manage the Exposition. The commission was to pay for many of the necessary buildings, to obtain state and county exhibits, and to keep an eye on the private businessmen who were running the show in Portland. Any disagreements between the commission and the company were to be referred to an arbitration committee of governor, secretary of state, and state treasurer. The end result, said the people's representatives in the rolling language of public bodies, would "benefit the people of the state of Oregon by way of the advertisement and development of the agricultural, horticultural, mineral, lumber, manufacturing, shipping, educational, and other resources of said state."

The emphasis on economic development set the theme for the more difficult lobbying job in Washington. No one in Congress had much interest in the historical heroes and their 2,000-mile trek. They did, however, share the same vision of Pacific trade that had motivated the exploration and settlement of the Oregon Country. Oregonians learned quickly in the winter of 1903-04 to cut the references to Lewis and Clark and to hammer home the idea that a Portland fair was "an undertaking of national interest and importance." With the help of testimony from the Washington and California delegations in Congress, they argued that the Exposition was a Pacific Coast enterprise that enjoyed the backing of chambers of commerce from San Diego to Spokane. Within the last few years, added W.L. Boise, the railroads had opened the door to the Northwest and laid its resources ready for development. The region's only remaining need was enough people to break the soil and fell the trees.

The perfect complement to the resources of the Northwest, said the same lobbyists, was the huge potential market of the Orient. Prineville's congressman, J.N. Williamson, requested export trade statistics for the Northwest states from Henry Reed in December. In hearings before the U.S. House Committee on Industrial Arts and Expositions held in January, 1904, Jefferson Myers of the state commission went straight to the point. "If all the wheat raised west of the Mississippi River were ground into flour for the Chinese trade," he told the panel, "the consumption per Chinaman would not exceeed one pancake per month." Harvey Scott had taken over the presidency of the Exposition Company after the death of Henry Corbett on March 31, 1903. He spoke the same day about the future of Pacific commerce in the practiced generalities of a journalistic booster. "That future is begun already," he concluded. "It is manifest, it presses, and it remains for us of America to seize it, to bear our part of it. We propose our exposition both as an incident and as an agent of this coming greatness."

In the meantime, unfortunately, Scott, Boise and Myers saw a thrifty Congress cut their original request by seventy-eight percent. The original bill introduced by Senator Dolliver of Iowa in December, 1903, called for federal authorization of the Exposition and an allocation of $2,125,000, a figure that the Senate trimmed by $400,000. The House was a more serious problem. Speaker Cannon was known to oppose further federal funding for expositions. Other congressmen were restless about the large appropriation for St. Louis's Louisiana Purchase Exposition and the pending request from the Jamestown Exposition. At House committee hearings on the Senate bill, Chairman James Tawney quickly established that the federal government did not need to authorize an exposition that the state of Oregon had already authorized. As a substitute for the Senate bill, Tawney and his colleagues issued a recommendation of $475,000 for both a government building and exhibits to illustrate the "administrative features of the Government in time of peace and its resources as a war power, thereby showing the nature of our institutions and their adaptation to the wants of the people."

To achieve the last step in the legislative process required all the political weight that Portlanders could throw. Oregon Senator John Mitchell had dispatched a flurry of letters and telegrams to make sure that a Portland delegation arrived in time for the Senate hearings in December and stayed over into the new year. As representatives of the Exposition Company, W.L. Boise, Oskar Huber, and especially Harvey Scott worked hard to open the federal treasury. Scott's sure touch with newspapermen and his stories of the Northwest told over brandy after marathon meals helped to set the right tone. His political alliance with Theodore Roosevelt was even more valuable. In January, J.N. Williamson reported that "President Roosevelt is helping us in every proper way." When the House balked at considering the aid bill in April, Scott made a second trip to Washington and asked the president's help in springing the bill for a vote on the floor. As Henry Reed reconstructed the event at second hand and a quarter-of-a-century later, Roosevelt replied vigorously, "That shall be done. What else can I do for you?" Whether the pressure was open or subtle, the appropriation passed without a roll call on April 8, 1904.

When Roosevelt signed the federal aid bill on April 13, the Lewis and Clark Centennial and American Pacific Exposition and Oriental Fair had already invested two years in specific planning and preparation. The executive committee of the corporation had advertised for sealed bids for the Exposition site in the early spring of 1902. Landowners had until Saturday, May 3, 1902, to deliver their proposals to the company offices at 246 Washington Street. Each bid was to describe the size of the parcel, its distance from Fifth and Morrison, the terms of the lease, and the number of acres that might be donated to the city for a permanent park. The company also wanted information on streetcar service, water supply for drinking, irrigation and lakes, and any other advantages of the site.

More than a dozen locations deserved at least brief consideration (Ross Island, the Love tract near Piedmont Park and Woodlawn, the Knox and Abrams tract near the Portland Flouring Mills on the east side of the Willamette River, and the Fulton waterfront on the west side, all dropped out quickly because of lack of space or isolation). Three east side sites were more serious contenders. University Park* had sufficient open land and grand views, but required a long car ride. City View Park at Sellwood† contained 178 acres but also suffered from distance. Hawthorne Park‡ offered an undeveloped tract of twelve acres bounded by Ninth and Twelfth avenues, Belmont, and Hawthorne. This latter site enjoyed direct streetcar service across the Madison and Morrison bridges, pure water from the Bull Run reservoir, and "natural lagoons" along a shallow stream. An adjacent twenty acres were available in Ladd's Addition, which had been platted in the early 1890s but delayed in development because of disputes over the estate of William S. Ladd.

For the owners of Hawthorne Park, the Exposition was simply one of several possibilities for completing a successful land speculation. A half-page advertisement in the *Oregonian* in the summer of 1902 covered all the possibilities: "Forest Trees 15 Feet in Circumference and a Fresh Wa-

---

*Now north Portland site of the University of Portland.

†Now Sellwood Park. (Just below Sellwood Park, on the Willamette, Oaks Park opened in 1905 as a counter site to the Lewis and Clark Exposition.)

‡Now an area of warehouses and light industry.

This photograph of the future Exposition site was taken from Willamette Heights, looking northeast. Guild's Lake, more accurately a marshland—it was fed by runoff and seepage; the map (RIGHT) indicates that its depth rarely exceeded three feet—is separated from the Willamette River by a thin strip of land. With only this picture for reference, it might be difficult to anticipate a transformation that as early as February, 1905 would merit the following description by a visiting legislative committee: "For natural beauty of environment the Lewis and Clark Exposition has no rival in earlier fairs. The Exposition structures, gleaming ivory white in their coats of ornamental staff, nestle among the trees at the top of a slight elevation overlooking Guild's Lake and the Willamette River, while in the distance four snow-capped peaks lift their hoary heads above the horizon."

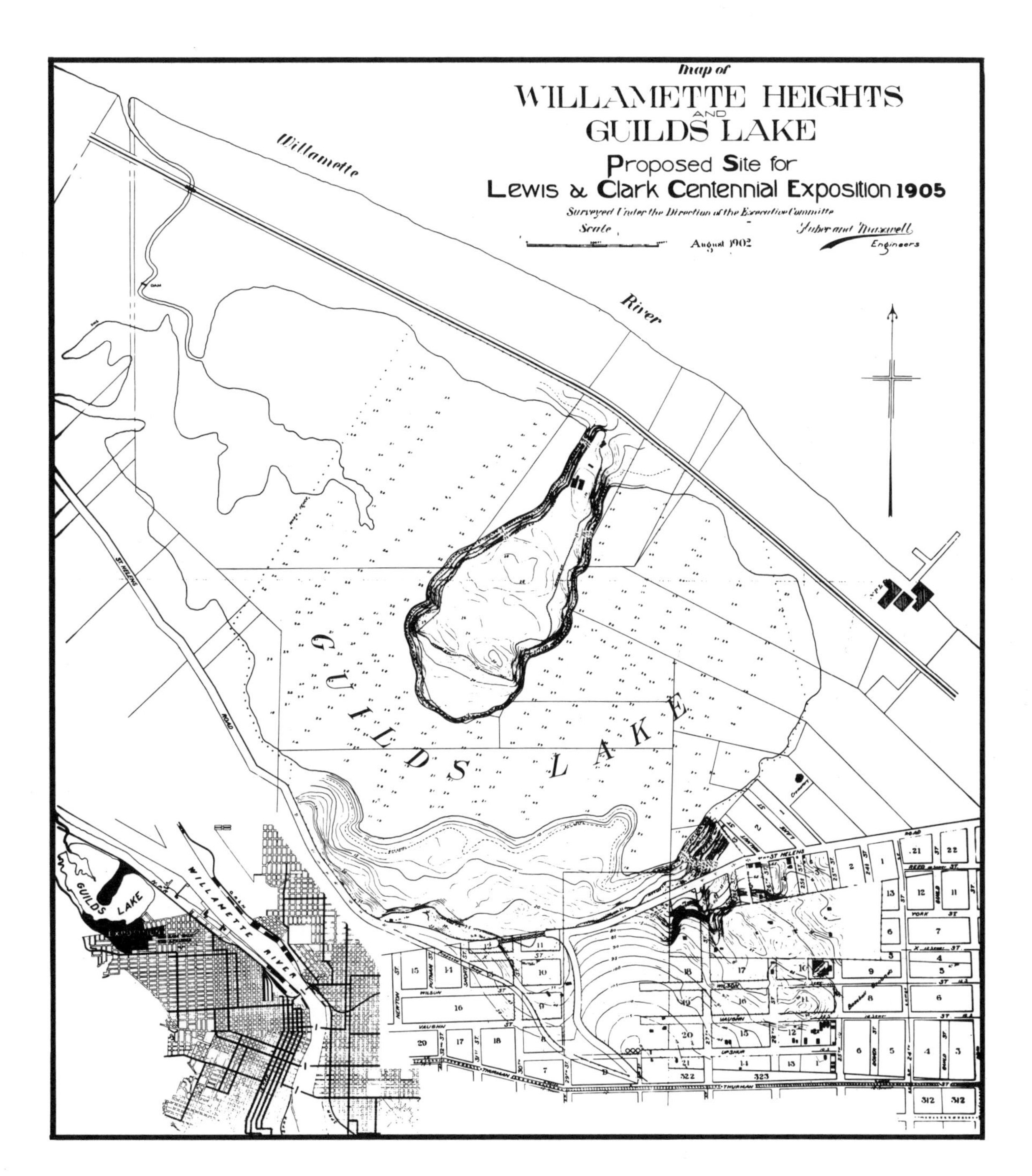
Map of
WILLAMETTE HEIGHTS
AND
GUILDS LAKE
Proposed Site for
Lewis & Clark Centennial Exposition 1905
Surveyed Under the Direction of the Executive Committee
Scale
August 1902
Huber and Maxwell
Engineers
Willamette
River
GUILDS LAKE
ST HELENS
ROAD
GUILDS LAKE
WILLAMETTE RIVER

ter Spring Spouts up to 1,500,000 Gallons Water Daily," proclaimed the headline. "This property is the logical location for the LEWIS AND CLARK CENTENNIAL EXPOSITION and the prettiest residential district in the United States," continued the copywriter. "The trees in the park have been growing since the water in the Willamette winkled in the sunlight or danced beneath the silvered face of the midnight moon." Potential purchasers were encouraged to consider either a giant flour mill powered by the "brooklet" or "a rural home within whistling distance of the business office."

City Park* was the initial west side competition. Its attractions were obvious—proximity to downtown hotels, public ownership of the land and planned improvements. The equally obvious disadvantage was the difficulty of providing streetcar service up its steep hillside. Indeed, a subcommittee of the Exposition Company voted for City Park in July, 1902 but reopened debate when the trolley companies refused to spend the $300,000 necessary to extend their lines. The suggestion of Guild's Lake as an alternative provided a graceful excuse for the reconsideration.

The new alternative covered 400 acres beyond the edge of settlement in northwest Portland. The road to the town of St. Helens followed the edge of a low bluff that crossed the south end of the site. The remainder of the area consisted of marshland, market gardens, and a dairy farm on a peninsula that extended into the "lake" itself. The Portland Railway and City and Suburban Railway companies ran cars within a block of the probable entrance, and the tracks of the Northern Pacific traced the eastern boundary. Although ownership was divided among more than forty parcels, the land was largely undeveloped and cheap to lease. Choice of the site also conveniently promised to benefit the new residential blocks of Willamette Heights, a development that was being promoted by Exposition board member Robert Livingstone.

The major concern that delayed a decision was confusion about Guild's Lake itself. Like Smith and Bybee lakes on the peninsula between the Columbia and Willamette, it was a shallow pan that filled with runoff and with seepage from the high water table. Although everyone in Portland was vaguely aware of the lake, no one on the site selection subcommittee could remember whether it evaporated during the dry season. An engineer's reconnaissance at the end of August, 1902, offered the necessary encouragement. The average depth in late summer was 2.5 feet and the maximum was 3.4 feet. The lake also was effectively empounded by the embankment that the Northern Pacific had built in 1888, and it did not rise and fall with fluctuations in the Willamette. If one fourteen-foot outlet through the embankment were dammed, the water level could be maintained for small boats by pumping from the river.

On September 5, after one more site inspection of Hawthorne Park, the subcommittee took its final vote. Rufus Mallory favored University Park, Henry Corbett reiterated the advantages of City Park, and Harvey Scott spoke at length for Hawthorne Park, pointing out that the city could obtain a permanent park for southeast Portland by purchasing the improved tract after the Fair. The vote, however, was six to two in favor of Guild's Lake, with the two east side locations holding their lone advocates. The full board ap-

*Now Washington Park.

proved the action on September 12 and the Lewis and Clark Exposition had its site—a grove of trees, 180 acres of pasture, and 220 acres of waist-high stagnant water at the site's center.

The first task at Guild's Lake's swamp was to divide the firmament from the waters. Preliminary grading started with 1903's first warm days in February, but halted in April for the visit of John Olmsted of Brookline, Massachusetts. Son of Frederick Law Olmsted—who had designed New York's Central Park—and himself a noted landscape architect in the family firm, John Olmsted was in Portland on a dual mission. The city park board was paying $5,000 for Portland's first scheme for a city-wide park system. The Lewis and Clark Exposition was paying a second $5,000 for a site plan for the Fair. A joint meeting of the corporation and state commission on April 28 adopted the resulting sketch of building sites, grades, and landscaping. It placed the major exhibition halls on the ridge overlooking the lake, located the U.S. Government Building on the waterfront to the northwest, and reserved the peninsula that stuck into the lake from the northeast for stock barns and a half-mile figure-eight race track. A railway across the narrow portion of the kidney-shaped lake was to link the entrance plaza and the U.S. Government Building to the race course.

It was the job of Oskar Huber as director of works to translate Olmsted's plan into reality. Huber, with the help of his partner William Maxwell, spent the month of May drawing precise specifications. Grading for roads, building sites, and waterfront esplanades resumed in June and was finished by the end of the summer. Connections to the city water mains provided drinking water. A second set of pipes tapped the Willamette River for fire hoses, lawn sprinklers, and sanitation, and a pumping station poured twenty million gallons of fresh water into the lake every day. Crews from Portland Light and Power strung electric lines to power the Exposition's 100,000 light bulbs.

The formal layout of the Exposition recalled the "White City" of Chicago's 1893 fair. The same aesthetic values that motivated the civic art movement and the revival of L'Enfant's plan for the District of Columbia also formed Portland's taste for a grand and artistic fair. The central element of the design was a strong northwest axis oriented to views of the Willamette River and Mount St. Helens. The only major deviation from the original plan was the decision to place the U.S. Government Building on the peninsula, where the twin towers tended to close the axis at the expense of a longer vista. Otherwise, the plan drew the visitor past the ionic columns at the gates and across Pacific Court to the sunken garden between the Palace of Agriculture and the Foreign Exhibits Building. Beyond the garden was Lake View Terrace and a grand staircase down the bluff to the bandstand, boat landing, and waterfront promenade. To the left, the entrance of the bridge to the peninsula was guarded by the amusements of The Trail, which were built on pilings over the lake.

The director of architecture was Ion Lewis, partner in the firm that dominated Portland design at the turn of the century, Whidden and Lewis. In a troublesome division of responsibilities, the corporation drew up plans and specifications under Lewis's supervision; the state commission ratified the plans, sent out for bids, and paid the bills out of the state appropriation. Testily rejecting a logical suggestion that the corpora-

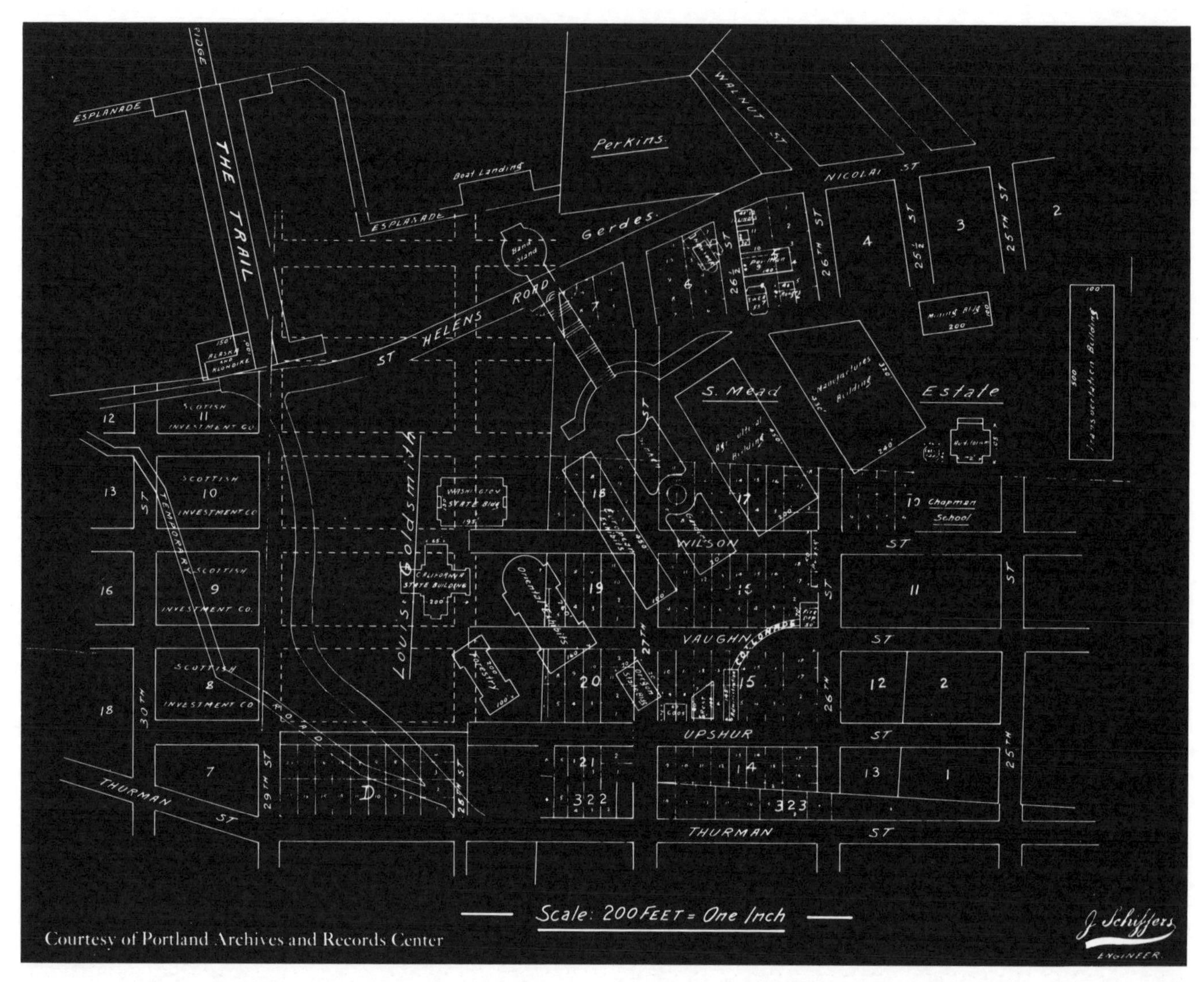

Courtesy of Portland Archives and Records Center

Layout of the Exposition (ABOVE) superimposed on a map of the area's existing streets and structures. It took only a few months to complete construction of the fairgrounds and buildings, commencement of which is documented by this photograph of the official ground-breaking party—a group that included (at the far right) Harvey W. Scott, an earlier president of the Exposition, and the former president of the Oregon Historical Society (LOWER RIGHT); on February 4, 1905, the day the Washington State Commission broke ground for its building (UPPER RIGHT), an Oregon legislative committee investigating the site reported that the state-funded building construction was almost complete.

tion itself act as general contractor, the commission opened bids for the individual buildings on March 19, 1904, and awarded the bulk of the business to Robert Wakefield, J.E. Bennett, and Burrell Construction. It also duplicated Lewis's job by hiring Fred A. Erixon, for $200 per month, to keep an eye on the progress of construction and landscaping. The buildings themselves cost only seventy-nine cents a square foot, for they were mostly plaster skins over wooden frames.

The structures matched the setting. The overall effect of the white-washed buildings grouped between river, lake, and hills was impressive: "a diamond set in a coronet of emeralds," in the words of Mayor Williams. Taken one by one, however, even local boosters had to admit that "the exhibition buildings are for the most part conventional in type." Portland's leading architects had drawn lots for the major structures: Oriental Exhibits to Emil Schacht; Foreign Exhibits to David Lewis; Palace of Agriculture to Edgar Lazarus; Administration Building to Henry J. Hefty; Mines and Metallurgy, Machinery-Electricity-Transportation, Festival Hall, Forestry, and the Oregon Building all to Whidden and Lewis. With one exception, the results followed the agreed style of "Spanish Renaissance," with domes, cupolas, arched doorways, and roofs covered with red tile or red paint. The main U.S. Government Building and the ancillary buildings for exhibits of fisheries, irrigation, a life-saving station, and the Pacific territories were designed by James Knox Taylor, architect of the U.S. Treasury. Rather than the post offices with classical facades that he often provided for his federal employer, he matched the eclecticism of the grouping on the bluff by crossing a railroad terminal with a Mexican cathedral.

The Forestry Building (the "largest log cabin in the world") was the anomaly, standing out like a logger at a toney party, scrubbed and shaved but still wearing a wool jacket in a room of tails and starched shirts. Located to the side of the grounds, where it would not break the formalism of the design, it was a huge log cabin of the sort no pioneer had ever built. In February, 1904, lumberman Simon Benson signed a contract for materials that specified "sound live timber with bark in perfect condition." The fir logs were to be cut "before the sap runs." Benson was to deliver them by rail if cut in Oregon or by raft up the Willamette if cut in Washington. A supplemental contract on June 30 allowed Burrell Construction $5,000 for wrestling the logs from Guild's Lake up to the building site (using a special quarter-mile chute) and for repairing the bark. The building itself stretched 105 feet by 209, fronted by a portico of natural tree trunks. The interior copied the nave of a church, with marching columns of tree trunks supporting the high ceiling and setting off the exhibition galleries and balconies along the sides. The largest foundation logs weighed thirty-two tons and measured fifty-four feet in length by five feet across. "Reduced to the exact reality of figures," said the New York *Review of Reviews*, "there was used in its building two miles of five-foot and six-foot fir logs, eight miles of poles, and many tons of shakes and cedar shingles."

If politics and planning were two keys to the preparation of the Lewis and Clark Exposition, the third was publicity. By the start of the twentieth century, the job of advertising a world's fair—of "exploiting" its possibilities—was an elaborate undertaking with a battery of techniques that were passed from city to city. At the head of the Division of Exploitation, Henry Reed spent $114,000 on a two-year campaign. Portland could not compete directly with the attention given to St. Louis during 1904, but the company could lay in the ammunition for the next year's publicity blitz. It prepared a 100-page book on Oregon and printed 300,000 copies. It persuaded the Portland post office to cancel outgoing mail with "World's Fair 1905." It rented space for information offices in Los Angeles, San Francisco, and Seattle. It dispatched J.P. Marshall, as special commissioner of the Division of Exploitation, to crisscross the West. At every town from the Pacific to the high plains he shared worn-down hotels with traveling salesmen, showed lantern slides to the chambers of commerce, and gladhanded to editors of the weekly papers.

By Reed's own estimate, the Division of Exploitation helped to secure more than 250,000 columns of newspaper space. There were 10,000 papers on the mailing list by the mid-point of the Fair; more than 6,000 received a weekly packet of features and photographs on western history, Oregon's resources, and Portland. Most of the stories were ready to drop into those painful gaps between the church news and the ads for sovereign remedies that haunted the days of small town editors. The company's writers provided "exclusives" on request and, from June to October 1905, one staff member worked full time to supply a daily report for the Associated Press. During the course of the summer, reporters and photographers used a total of 50,000 free Exposition admissions. The Union Pacific, the Southern Pacific, and the Northern Pacific railroads also helped by printing their own flyers and taking out their own advertising to push their special rates for fairgoers.

Beyond the customary media, Portland enjoyed a unique opportunity to publicize its own fair at the Louisiana Purchase Exposition in St. Louis. Along with $450,000 for use in Portland, the Oregon legislature in 1903 appropriated $50,000 for the state's participation in St. Louis. The job of erecting Oregon's building and organizing the exhibits fell to Jefferson Myers and the Lewis and Clark Centennial Exposition Commission. The St. Louis management cooperated by granting Oregon a site near the center of the grounds between the Fine Arts and the United States buildings, rather than in the far corner with most of the other state buildings. Fir and pine were cut to specifications in Oregon and shipped across country to be assembled into a replica of Fort Clatsop (where Lewis and Clark and their companions took shelter from the winter of 1805-06 at the mouth of the Columbia).

Oregon's exhibits cost exactly $23,568 to assemble and display and $1,448 for rail freight. In addition to its own building, the commission filled nearly 8,000 square feet of exhibit space in the Education, Mining, Fisheries, Agriculture, Horticulture and Forestry halls with a hodgepodge of materials donated by Oregon businesses, farmers and ranchers. According to detailed shipping lists, the Forestry Building exhibit included one pair of elk horn, twenty pieces of wood, twenty-nine bundles of plants, pine cones, two polished alder burls, one black oak burl, and so on through page after page. It also included consignments from West Coast Sash and Door Company, Star Box Company, Jones Lumber Company and Multnomah Trunk and Box Company. Visitors to Oregon's horticulture exhibit found prunes, and more prunes—six tons of them had filled Southern Pacific car 66124.

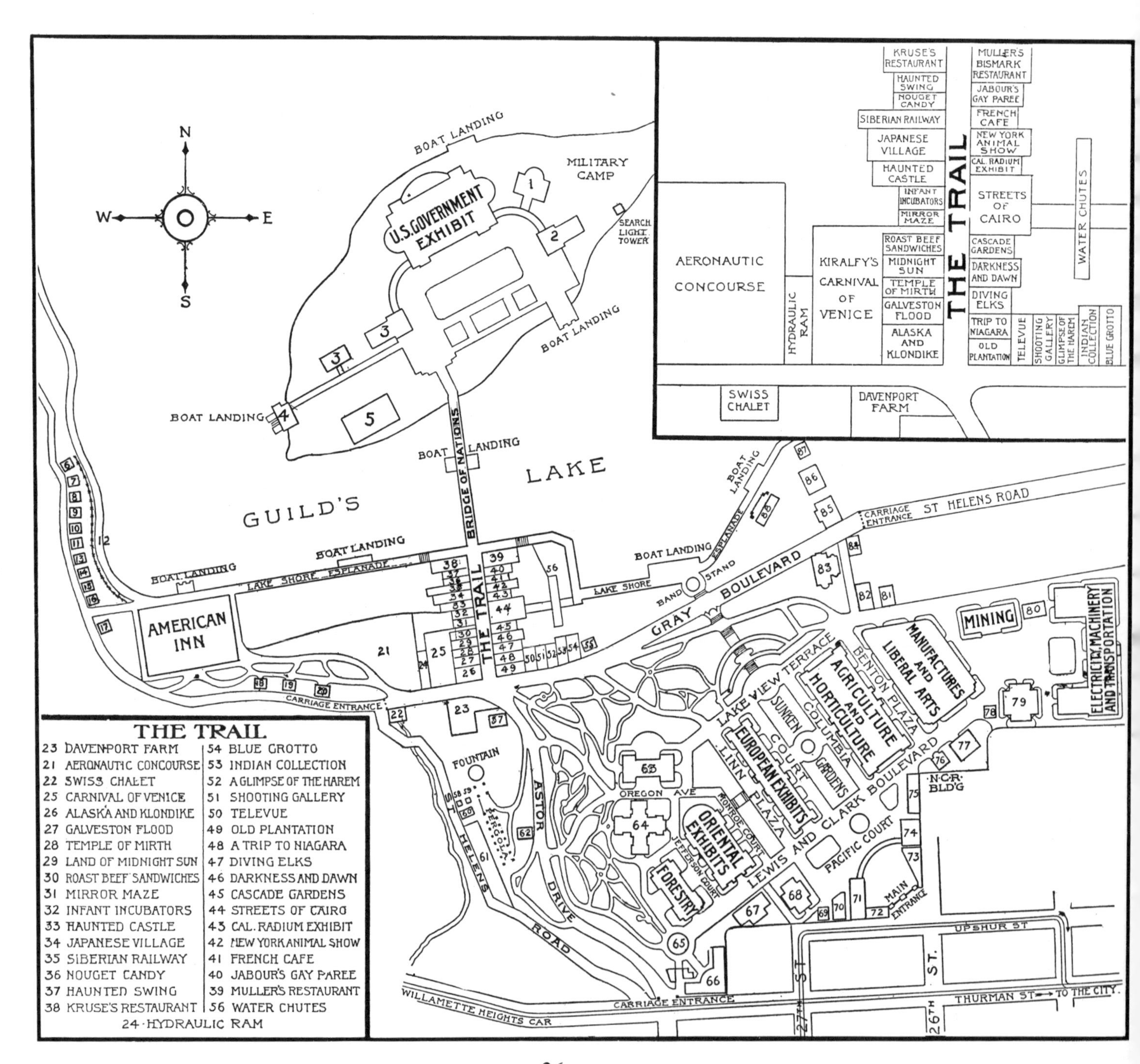
THE TRAIL
23 DAVENPORT FARM
21 AERONAUTIC CONCOURSE
22 SWISS CHALET
25 CARNIVAL OF VENICE
26 ALASKA AND KLONDIKE
27 GALVESTON FLOOD
28 TEMPLE OF MIRTH
29 LAND OF MIDNIGHT SUN
30 ROAST BEEF SANDWICHES
31 MIRROR MAZE
32 INFANT INCUBATORS
33 HAUNTED CASTLE
34 JAPANESE VILLAGE
35 SIBERIAN RAILWAY
36 NOUGET CANDY
37 HAUNTED SWING
38 KRUSE'S RESTAURANT
54 BLUE GROTTO
53 INDIAN COLLECTION
52 A GLIMPSE OF THE HAREM
51 SHOOTING GALLERY
50 TELEVUE
49 OLD PLANTATION
48 A TRIP TO NIAGARA
47 DIVING ELKS
46 DARKNESS AND DAWN
45 CASCADE GARDENS
44 STREETS OF CAIRO
43 CAL. RADIUM EXHIBIT
42 NEW YORK ANIMAL SHOW
41 FRENCH CAFE
40 JABOUR'S GAY PAREE
39 MULLER'S RESTAURANT
56 WATER CHUTES
24 HYDRAULIC RAM
N
S
W
E
U.S. GOVERNMENT EXHIBIT
MILITARY CAMP
SEARCH LIGHT TOWER
BOAT LANDING
BRIDGE OF NATIONS
GUILD'S
LAKE
AMERICAN INN
LAKE SHORE ESPLANADE
LAKE SHORE
THE TRAIL
CARRIAGE ENTRANCE
ST HELENS ROAD
ESPLANADE
BAND STAND
GRAY BOULEVARD
MINING
MANUFACTURES AND LIBERAL ARTS
ELECTRICITY, MACHINERY AND TRANSPORTATION
AGRICULTURE AND HORTICULTURE
BENTON PLAZA
LAKE VIEW TERRACE
SUNKEN COURT
COLUMBIA GARDENS
EUROPEAN EXHIBITS
LINN PLAZA
ORIENTAL EXHIBITS
FORESTRY
OREGON AVE
MONROE COURT
JEFFERSON COURT
LEWIS AND CLARK BOULEVARD
PACIFIC COURT
N.C.R. BLD'G
MAIN ENTRANCE
FOUNTAIN
ASTOR
DRIVE
ST HELENS
ROAD
UPSHUR ST
27TH ST
26TH ST
THURMAN ST → TO THE CITY
WILLAMETTE HEIGHTS CAR
KRUSE'S RESTAURANT
HAUNTED SWING
NOUGET CANDY
SIBERIAN RAILWAY
JAPANESE VILLAGE
HAUNTED CASTLE
INFANT INCUBATORS
MIRROR MAZE
ROAST BEEF SANDWICHES
MIDNIGHT SUN
TEMPLE OF MIRTH
GALVESTON FLOOD
ALASKA AND KLONDIKE
MULLER'S BISMARK RESTAURANT
JABOUR'S GAY PAREE
FRENCH CAFE
NEW YORK ANIMAL SHOW
CAL. RADIUM EXHIBIT
STREETS OF CAIRO
CASCADE GARDENS
DARKNESS AND DAWN
DIVING ELKS
TRIP TO NIAGARA
OLD PLANTATION
TELEVUE
SHOOTING GALLERY
GLIMPSE OF THE HAREM
INDIAN COLLECTION
BLUE GROTTO
WATER CHUTES
AERONAUTIC CONCOURSE
HYDRAULIC RAM
KIRALFY'S CARNIVAL OF VENICE
SWISS CHALET
DAVENPORT FARM

LEWIS AND CLARK CENTENNIAL AND AMERICAN PACIFIC EXPOSITION AND ORIENTAL FAIR PORTLAND, OREGON —— 1905

H. W. GOODE, President   OSCAR HUBER, Director Works

STATE BUILDINGS.
64 CALIFORNIA
78 COLORADO
85 IDAHO
84 ILLINOIS
67 MASSACHUSETTS
77 MISSOURI
83 NEW YORK
68 OREGON
86 UTAH
63 WASHINGTON

U. S. GOVERNMENT EXHIBIT
Wings to Main Exhibit Building
1 FORESTRY AND IRRIGATION
2 ALASKA AND PHILIPPINES
3 FISH COMMISSION
4 LIFE-SAVING STATION

MISCELLANEOUS
6 WINSTACKER
7 WINDMILLS
8 HYDRAULIC GRAVEL ELEVATOR
9-10 STUMP PULLERS
11 YOKES
12 ROAD OILING MACHINE
13 RAILWAY EQUIPMENT CO.
14 GASOLINE
15 TRACTION ENGINES
16 BEE DEPOSIT DETECTOR
17 DRILLS
55 PUMPING PLANT
57 DUTCH BAKERY
58 SEATTLE GIN SIN
59 McDOWELL GIN SIN
60 BURNS' COTTAGE
62 OLYMPIA BREWING CO.
65 WATER TOWER
66 FINE ARTS BUILDING
67 COOS COUNTY
70 RESTAURANT
71 ADMINISTRATION BUILDING
72 PRESS
73 POST OFFICE
74 FIRE DEPARTMENT
75 PUBLIC COMFORT
76 NATIONAL CASH REGISTER
79 AUDITORIUM
80 GEOLOGICAL BUILDING
81 MAJESTIC STOVES
82 Y. W. C. A.
87 FRATERNAL TEMPLE
88 HUNGARIAN CSARDA

This map of the fairgrounds (LEFT) was printed in the center of the daily programs received by visitors with their admission tickets.

The allocation of exhibits was in fact a point of controversy. W.H. Wehrung, superintendent of agriculture, horticulture and forestry for the Lewis and Clark Exposition, and who supervised the Oregon effort in St. Louis, had strongly urged that all the state's displays be consolidated in Fort Clatsop. The state commission had decided to the contrary, distributing the exhibits among the various open departments of the exposition in the hope of piling up a high score of medals and prizes. Also, lack of advertising literature presented a problem. With its central location, Oregon's building received more than 1,000,000 visitors, but only 165,000 brochures were available to last the entire summer. In his final report, Wehrung circumspectly noted that Oregon pamphlets were so rare that they never appeared in the fair's wastebaskets. Henry Dosch, who represented the Lewis and Clark Exposition Company in St. Louis, was more blunt in one of his letters to the Portland office. Not only had the state commission been too cheap to publish its own literature, he reported, but Jefferson Myers had even refused a shipment of booklets published by the corporation because he did not want to pay the freight.

Disagreements among the state commissioners and their assistants came to a climax in the hot and sticky days in mid-June, when Dosch was wishing plaintively for "a good breath of Oregon air and a drink of Bull Run water—it beats Schlitz." On June 15, the state commission had dedicated the building and hosted a lunch for 900 people with expenses of $53.50 for "mints, cake, and almonds" and $50.00 for peonies (at a dollar a dozen). The "wine, berries, champagne and pineapples" (at $24.62) may have drowned people's better judgement. Wehrung may have been an-

There are few obvious clues here to suggest that this warehouse harbored exotic contents. The only major American contribution to the building was its construction materials; built by Robert Wakefield Company of Portland, the Liberal Arts, or Foreign Exhibits, Building (the former its contract name, the latter used during the fair) housed exhibits from Italy, Russia, Hungary, Austria, France, Switzerland, Holland and the British Empire.

This edifice, the federal government's contribution to the Exposition, was designed by United States Architect James Knox Taylor. The fair's largest exhibit building, its central structure occupied 74,800 square feet and was connected by 200-foot-long colonnades (one of which can be seen at the center of this view) with two auxiliary buildings, each 100x100 feet. The U.S. Government Building was situated on the peninsula that jutted into the center of Guild's Lake from the Willamette side; it could be reached from mainland by crossing the Bridge of Nations or via ferryboat. Construction began late in 1904; this photograph was taken on January 9, 1905.

By March 11, 1905, two months after the preceding photograph (p. 29) was taken, the colonnade had been relieved of its scaffolding and workmen were installing the wooden walkway. Despite Portland's wet spring weather, building construction on the mainland was also proceeding apace, to meet the June 1 deadline.

And in less than three weeks the walkway, complete save for a few wayward ladders and odd scraps of lumber, was ready to receive visitors. Only three months later, Vice President Charles Fairbanks would inspect buildings connected by this colonnade, filled with federal exhibits, on opening day.

Northwest of the Sunken Gardens and Lake View Terrace (see map, page 26), fairgoers could descend a terraced slope to the lakefront via the Grand Stairway, seen here close to completion. At its foot stood the Grand Bandstand, at which point the stairway intersected the Lake Shore Esplanade. Here also, from a landing beyond the bandstand, boats shuttled fairgoers to the U.S. Government Building, or moored between cruises around the lake.

A study in contrast, the Forestry Building, described as the largest log cabin in the world, and the elegant Oriental Exhibits rose side by side. Both were funded by the state of Oregon; both were completed relatively early in the construction process. The Oregon Building (foreground), also funded by the state and designed to fit with the central grouping's "Spanish Renaissance" style, faced the other two buildings across Lewis and Clark Boulevard.

LIBERAL ARTS

Standing near the Fair entrance, Oregon's state building (ABOVE) served primarily as an information and administration center, with a reception area, offices and public accommodation rooms. The state commission hosted exhibits in the Palace of Agriculture, and the Mines, Forestry, Oriental and Coos County buildings. The Oregon Building was one of five state-funded structures designed by the Portland architectural firm of Whidden and Lewis.

Of the nine European nations exhibiting in the Liberal Arts (Foreign Exhibits) Building (LEFT), Italy was allotted the largest space, and filled it with statuary and paintings, leather, shell and handworked textile products, and agricultural products. Russia, with one of the smallest exhibits, offered perhaps the most diverse collection of goods: samovars, oriental sweets, cement, preserved meats, wines, chemicals, graphic arts and books, and smoked sausages.

The Exposition's central vista stretched from its entrance gates, over the Sunken Gardens and down the Grand Stairway to the U.S. Government Building across the Bridge of Nations. The Foreign Exhibits Building (at left) and the Agriculture and Horticulture Palace (to the right) bordered this view. Wide walkways, marble statuary and elegant planters accented the buildings' classical façades and the formal layout; every element of the landscape contributed to the magical grandeur that marks a great extravaganza.

noyed past caution by comparing the cost of the party with his own tight entertainment budget. At any event, the outcome was a tremendous row among the state commissioners, the general superintendent, and the assistant superintendents who guarded the scattered Oregon exhibits. According to Dosch's gleeful report, there nearly were blows between Wehrung and two commissioners, Frank Williams of Ashland and E.D. Young of the University of Oregon. Although Wehrung stuck out his job to the end of the fall, many of the original assistants had to be replaced by mid-summer.

The Lewis and Clark Exposition was a civic responsibility as well as a business enterprise. Advertising for the Fair supplied Portlanders an opportunity to boost the growth of their city and state. As early as 1902, the Portland Board of Trade used an article by J.M. Long on "Portland's World Fair" to open the first volume of its new *Columbia River Basin Journal: Devoted to the Development, Advancement, and Progress of the Pacific Northwest.* In January, 1904, W.S. Duniway introduced the first issue of the *Lewis and Clark Journal* by stating his intent to show the sectional and national character of the Exposition by focusing on the history, growth, and prospects of the Northwest. In the fall, lagging subscriptions forced the *Lewis and Clark Journal* under the "fostering care" of the corporation and the editorial hand of D.C. Freeman, but the monthly issues continued to cover the progress of the Fair, the attractions of Portland as a tourist town, regional history, Northwest Indians, and the scenery and resources of Oregon. For example, the decision to erect a special Coos County Building sparked a plethora of pieces on North Bend and Coos Bay.

The modern reader might be more surprised at the coverage of the Exposition in the *Pacific Monthly.* Editor William B. Wells had made the Portland magazine a vehicle for regional literature and had developed a sophisticated audience for stories by Jack London and essays by John Muir. During 1905, the same subscribers could read about "The Lewis and Clark Exposition" in January, "State and Foreign Participation in the Lewis and Clark Exposition" in February, "Progress of the Lewis and Clark Exposition" in March, and "Oregon's Log Palace" in April. In Wells's own opinion, the attention was perfectly in line with his journal's role as a spokesman for the West:

> *At no time during the last century had the Pacific Coast such an opportunity for showing the world the vast possibilities and opportunities for individual, collective and national advancement as that which is to be presented to the Coast immediately preceding and during the period of the Lewis and Clark Fair. The Exposition to be held in Portland represents the culmination of the various agencies and activities which have been working together during the past two decades to draw the attention of the world to this section . . . the Lewis and Clark Fair strikes the iron while it is hot, and, . . .brings the publicity of the various agencies to a full fruition. Only a dullard could be blind, therefore, to the tremendous and overwhelming opportunity which is offered in the way of advertising to the Pacific Coast States.* (February 1905, p. 142)

Publicity for the Exposition in local and national magazines added up to an informal self-portrait of the ideal Portland. The planning for a regional exposition reconfirmed what Portlanders already knew about their city. "The title of Portland to be the seat of so important an undertaking," said the managing editor of the *Oregonian*, "rests on the fact that it has been for more than fifty years the chief city of the Pacific Northwest." Most residents assumed that Portland's preeminence in the industrial life of the Northwest was beyond debate. In particular, it seemed obvious that the city's bankers and wholesalers dominated the financial life of Oregon and Washington. Portland was not merely a "neighborhood center," Albert Holman told the readers of *World's Work*, but a city like Atlanta, New Orleans, St. Paul, or San Francisco that served as the headquarters of an entire region.

Future growth for the city seemed assured by its location, for Portland was the natural gateway between the Columbia Valley's agriculture and the vast markets of the Orient and Latin America. Time and again, Portlanders talked about lumber and wheat, flour and lumber, lumber and grain. They pointed to the new twenty-seven-foot channel to the Pacific and to the water-level route to the interior that assured ultimate success over Seattle and Tacoma. In the early years of this century, the illustration chosen for most articles on Portland was a photograph looking north from the Steel Bridge over a harbor crowded with rafts of logs and dozens of grain ships.

The principal city of the Northwest was also the region's "most substantial" in the eyes of its residents. According to an article in the *Pacific Monthly*, it was "well-built and metropolitan in appearance . . . in every respect an Eastern city." Here, "eastern" meant modern. Portland streets were clean and paved and brightly lighted and lined with shade trees. Its hotels were distinguished. Its business was conducted in modern and convenient buildings and its streetcar system was as good as any other city's. An "eastern" city was also a refined city where visitors need not fear the crudity of the pioneer West. Portlanders were proud of their wealth, their numerous millionaires, and the "momentum of stored riches" that made respectability the local watchword. Householders enjoyed fine homes and the "cozy quality" of their town. Schools, libraries, newspapers and art museum represented the "ease of a matured civilization" and convinced residents that they lived in the "social and economic center" as well as the economic metropolis of the Northwest.

Seal of the Lewis and Clark Centennial and American Pacific Exposition and Oriental Fair, celebrating the one-hundredth anniversary of the explorations of the Oregon Country by captains Meriwether Lewis and William Clark.

III

The Wonderful Summer

Excitement about the Lewis and Clark Exposition picked up as winter began to soften into the spring of 1905. When the gates clanged shut at St. Louis, national interest turned to Portland. Scores of carpenters, groundskeepers and other employees of the Louisiana Purchase Exposition bought tickets west, hoping for another year of work. Dozens of small entrepreneurs made the same trip looking for properties to rent and operate as boarding houses. Two other participants in the same migration moved directly into the executive offices of the Exposition Company. Theodore Hardee had been assistant to the secretary of the Louisiana Purchase Exposition and stepped into the same position as chief assistant to Henry Goode, who had followed Harvey Scott as company president in August, 1904. The new director of concessions and admissions was John A. Wakefield, an exposition veteran who had worked at Omaha and assisted the director of concessions at St. Louis.

The growing staff at the Exposition headquarters had to sort through five hundred mail inquiries every day. Dozens of young ladies wanted to spend the summer in Portland as a company stenographer. Scores of young men offered their credentials as guards or messengers. Senators and congressmen assumed that their vote for the Fair gave them the right to recommend their constituents for Portland jobs, and the management did its best to please these legislators. A letter from William Loeb, secretary to Theodore Roosevelt, described the virtues of E.S. Kinkaid, who had served in the president's own regiment during the Spanish-American War, and who turned out to be perfectly suited to the Exposition's needs.

Correspondence from bands and soloists who wanted to provide the musical entertainment grew to a pile nearly a foot high. Matus and his Royal Hungarian Court Orchestra wrote from Brooklyn. Carl Riedelsberger, dean of music at Montana College, wrote from Deer Lodge. The Boston Letter Carriers Band wrote from the Hub. Also from New England were Helen May Butler and her Ladies Military Brass Band. Ms. Butler looked competent and charming in the publicity photo that accompanied her application, with short blond hair curling out from under her shako, but she, as most of the applicants, failed to secure employment. Four bands were engaged for periods of four to six weeks. The Innes Band performed in June, Liberati's Band in July, the troublesome Royal Hawaiian Band in August and Sepember, and Ellery's Royal Italians (despite the name, they were Chicago Italians to a man) played through the last week.

John Wakefield was equally swamped with applications for concessions. A drugstore owner in Nebraska wanted the root beer franchise. Another entrepreneur offered designs for the world's most elaborate soda fountain. Day after day, Wakefield made mental notes, dashed off quick replies, and dropped the morning's mail into file folders. By May he had selected a total of seventy-six souvenir sellers, fifteen ice cream and soft drink stands, and a dozen restaurants. There would be cookies at the Dutch Bakery, German sausage at Muller's, roast beef sandwiches at a stand along The Trail, and cold beer at the Swiss Chalet operated by the Olympia Brewing Company.

During the same busy months of March and April, someone in the Exposition's office presumably read the entries in the poetry contest. The theme was "The Trail" and the poems came in by the hundreds. Most rhymed and loped, in a dogtrot, from line to line. With an occasional oddity, they were historical, uplifting and irredeemable. The first stanzas from a Hood River entry capture the tone;

In days of yore, in time grown olden,
When this fair land gave chances golden,
There lay embedded in each breast
A bold desire to move out west.

And as a place of destiny
Our fathers sought this empire free,
Where rolls the Oregon in might
And nature blessed all things in sight.

When the city settled back from the rush of opening day, it was clear that Portland was a rare specimen—an exposition city equipped to handle its visitors. Fairgoers with a thick wallet could lodge at the American Inn on the Exposition grounds, where 585 convenient rooms cost $1.50 to $5.00 on the European plan and $4.00 to $7.00 American plan. There were another 5,000 rooms within walking distance, in boarding houses and in the score of new two-story or three-story frame hotels like the Detroit, the Fairmount, and the Outside Inn. Other space was available in private homes and in the established hotels downtown. The Exposition Accommodation Bureau in the Goodnough Building at Fifth and Yamhill maintained lists of rooms at "reasonable rates" and handled advance reservations. From the central business district, fairgoers would catch the Portland Railway streetcars on Washington Street or the City and Suburban cars on Morrison for the twenty-minute ride. For a dime they could board a steamer for a ride down the Willamette to the U.S. Government Building.

Tourists found a set of exhibits that had taken three years to assemble. In 1903, Henry Goode had visited New York, Washington and St. Louis to persuade foreign governments that Portland would provide a perfect follow-up to St. Louis. The company also spent $4,500 to send Henry Dosch with the same message to the Osaka fair of 1903 and staked his expenses for six months at the Louisiana Purchase Exposition. He later claimed to have rejected 250 exhibitors, but as late as October, 1904, he was sending discouraging reports about the reluctance of American corporations to crate their exhibits and ship them west. Since the Portland Exposition was not officially authorized by Congress, the U.S. State Department was reluctant to issue formal invitations to foreign governments. For practical assistance, however, the Treasury Department did declare the fairgrounds a bonded warehouse so that foreign goods could be displayed without payment of import duties.

Japan's million-dollar exhibit made the most impressive showing among the twenty-one nations that participated. Its cases of silks, porcelains and lanterns matched the theme of the American Pacific Exposition and Oriental Fair. The adjacent European Building displayed the achievements of the industrial age. With their stunning defeat by Japan at the naval battle of Tsushima Strait less than a week old when the Exposition opened, the Russian representatives must have wondered about the real differences between the modern West and picturesque East when they stared at the Oriental Building across Linn Plaza.

Many visitors preferred the exhibits that explained the progress and resources of Oregon and its neighbors. The Omaha, St. Louis and Buffalo fairs all had had player pianos and buggies and displays of dental drills. Only Portland had the Forestry Building with its pine cone decorations, samples of lumber, and dioramas of elk and panthers, not to mention the American Indians photographs of Edward Curtis. The mining exhibit included a miniature mountain and mine. The United States exhibit on the peninsula boasted working models of the Salt River and Palouse River projects of the Reclamation Service. There were panoramas of the Grand Canyon and Yellowstone Falls, an aquarium and hatchery, and totem poles from Haida and Tlingit villages on Prince of Wales Island.

Fairgoers carried their taste for the scientific and the educational across the Bridge of Nations from the United States exhibit to The Trail. No one bothered with the amusements that were matched at any carnival—the Mirror Maze, the Haunted Swing. The fairgoers preferred three dimensional copies of the *National Geographic*; the Streets of Cairo and the Siberian Railroad repeating their success at St. Louis. Real science was represented by the Infant Incubators. According to Oelo McClay, from Coos County:

> *There was six young babies there, kept in glass cases on pillows or beds laid on springs . . . the whole case for each baby is about two feet by three. There was two rooms, one for the very young babies and one for them when they are a few months older. There they keep them in a cooler atmosphere and teach them to take artificial food from a bottle and can soon be sent home a strong and healthy baby.*

The most elaborate concession was Bolossy Kiralfy's Carnival of Venice, whose performances required a 400-foot stage and a cast of hundreds (half of them ballet dancers from Europe,

Washington's Chelan County, encompassing mountainous and rolling land in the north central part of the state, was established in 1899, six years before the Exposition gates opened. Part of a collective 16-county exhibit in the Washington State Building, the colorful display enticed visitors with a lavish spread of fruits and vegetables native to the area, while scenic wall murals portrayed the region's abundant geographical and natural resources.

The Post Office Department, exhibiting in the U.S. Government Building, boasted a complete collection of U.S. postage stamps dating from their introduction in 1847, stamped envelopes dating from 1853, and foreign stamps. Examples of postal equipment, including an international collection of mailboxes and uniformed manikins of the mailcarriers who emptied them, were also on display, as were items related to postal transportation and history. The department's dead letter collection, comprised of lost and confiscated goods, included paintings, Indian relics, deadly weapons, poisonous reptiles and "opium and other articles of like character."

In 1905, fairgoers crowded into the huge structure of the Forestry Building, which was filled with wildlife dioramas and Oregon's forest products. The exhibits, arranged simply, matched the mood of the building; they were enclosed by railings similar to those visible at the balcony level. One of the feature attractions was a display of nine-foot-wide planks hewn from a single tree. The state fish commission exhibited here as well, and a collection of about 300 Edward S. Curtis photographs of North American Indians adorned the walls.

In the Government Building the U.S. Navy exhibited an assortment of models that included navy vessels (at 1/48th actual size), a 30x9-foot working drydock at which a miniature U.S.S. *Illinois* docked and undocked daily, and a model of the U.S. Naval Academy at Annapolis. The department's ordnance division assembled for display an array of naval armaments, and, on a 12x18-foot screen in a 200-seat theater, a daily feature of 60 biograph motion scenes (projected in sequences of 10 or 12) depicted the excitement of navy life.

Complete with serenading gondoliers and scheming lovers who drifted between audience and stage, Bolossy Kiralfy's 400-foot-long set recalled Venice's Grand Canal during the height of that legendary city's gay carnival season. The carnival's 300 members, including a large contingent of European ballerinas and a chorus drawn from the Metropolitan Opera Company, entertained fairgoers with dances, songs and skits.

Every fair has its amusement park, and the Lewis and Clark Exposition had The Trail. According to its official souvenir book, a trip through The Trail was accompanied by "boisterous noise of brass music," and "a succession of discordant crashes which distracted attention from many a less presuming attraction behind high walls. Scenic and electrical illusions abound, trained animals there are, wonderful things displayed and frightful happenings enacted." The numerous and colorful "ballyhoos," supposedly attracting fairgoers to admission events, were described as "frequently having no relevancy to anything but promiscuous and conscienceless advertising."

In the center of the fairgrounds, between the Palace of Agriculture and the Foreign Exhibits Building, the spacious lawn of the Sunken Gardens provided visitors a relaxing oasis. Musical diversion might emanate from a stage at the gardens' center, or perhaps waft up from the Bandstand at lakefront. Stretching from the fair's entrance colonnade to Lake View Terrace overlooking the Grand Stairway, the gardens were bordered by expansive walkways and elaborate electric lights; this section of the grounds harbored many of the Exposition's statues, including that sculpted by Alice Cooper of Sacajawea (later relocated to Portland's Washington Park).

Fairgoers walking along a section of the Lake Shore Esplanade. The Bandstand, the Grand Stairway, and the towering buildings on the upper tier of the Fair can be seen. The Esplanade bordered the Exposition's lake front, intersecting with the Bridge of Nations and continuing as far as the American Inn (see p. 26).

according to the press release). "Gondolas float between the audience and the stage, and the entertainment consists of dances, choruses, solos, marches, specialties, and tableaux, with a touch of comedy running through the performance."

An hour's worth of marches and tableaux may seem a bit much to our taste, but who could resist Professor Barnes's Educated Horse and Diving Elk? The two elk had eight years of experience at their odd profession of diving headlong into a tank of water from a forty-foot high ramp. Their travels had taken them to the corners of civilization—the great capitals of London, Paris, and Berlin, the expositions at Buffalo and Toronto, and through America to Cincinnati, Kansas City, and Coney Island. As part of the price of admission, Professor Barnes gave his horse, Princess Trixie, the chance to demonstrate her abilities. Equine intelligence—the command of language and arithmetic—had recently been displayed by Clever Hans in Berlin and Jim Key at the St. Louis fair, but Princess Trixie outperformed them both. "These elk are an example of what can be accomplished with wild animals through the kind and rational methods of training pursued by Professor Barnes," wrote the *Lewis and Clark Journal*. "Princess Trixie demonstrates to the most skeptical that the noble horse can be taught the English language and can think and reason the same as any human being."

The skepticism of the Exposition management did spare the public one other opportunity for an "entertaining and instructive spectacle." Early in June, former heavyweight boxing champion John L. Sullivan offered—demanded—to buy the space that had been assigned to the California Radium Exhibit. For more than a week, he deluged the concessions committee with telegrams, letters from congressmen, testimonials to his good character, and press releases from a previous appearance in Spokane. A decade out of the boxing ring and a decade fuller in the paunch, he proposed to don a white costume and wig and portray famous works of statuary in front of a purple velvet curtain. He had actually visited art galleries of the Old World and America, he assured John Wakefield, and the whole performance would include an uplifting narrative. Rejection of his offer may have driven Sullivan to one more bout of reform, for later in the year he foreswore the bottle and took to the boards as a temperance lecturer.

Though it rejected Sullivan's purple drapes, the Exposition did lay on a battery of special attractions for weekday visitors. The U.S. Government Building and the National Cash Register Pavillion (just inside the main entrance of the Fair) showed free motion pictures. A squadron of warships from Dewey's victorious Manila fleet tied up in the Willamette and offered free tours. Concerts in the lakefront bandstand were scheduled daily from 2:30 to 4:30 and later 8:00 to 10:00. When the Royal Hawaiian Band started to shorten its evening performance because of the cold, the concert was changed to 7:30 and, on September 4, moved indoors. On June 21, the winners of the first transcontinental auto race arrived at the fairgrounds to great fanfare; it had taken forty-four days for Dwight Huss and Milford Wright to drive their 800-pound Oldsmobile from Fifty-Ninth and Broadway in New York to Portland. Controlled by eighteen-year-old Lincoln Beachey, T.S. Baldwin's motor-driven blimps *Angelus* and *City of Portland* made nine ascents from the aeronautic concourse near the American Inn during August and September.

The boy aeronaut hung precariously below the gasbag in an open framework that carried an engine and propeller at one end and the steering vanes at the other. On one trip to Vancouver he ran into stiff Columbia River winds that blew him downstream nearly to Scappoose. His most spectacular flight was on September 26, when Beachey piloted the *City of Portland* over the business district, touched down on the roof of the Chamber of Commerce Building, and returned to the Fair after a fifty-five minute trip.

Sunday was a special problem. In response to the strong national lobby for Sunday closings, the Fair management planned to open the gates on Sundays but turn off the machinery in the exhibits and padlock the amusements. Fairgoers could still enjoy the wooded paths and lakeshore promenades, attend special concerts of sacred music, and profit from lectures by noted clergymen such as Josiah Strong of the League for Social Service and Newell Dwight Hillis of Brooklyn's famous Plymouth Church. With lagging attendance and receipts, however, the concessioners of The Trail secured an injunction on July 30 that allowed them to open seven days a week. Reporting in retrospect, Henry Reed claimed that after the injunction Portlanders had refused the seduction of Sunday entertainment in favor of church services and family picnics.

The high-minded visitor unsated by Sunday sermons could also attend special conferences on education, civics, Indian affairs, industrial relations and the United States' future in the Orient. Speakers included professors from the University of California at Berkeley, Harvard, Dartmouth, Columbia and the universities of Pennsylvania and Wisconsin. Thirty-four national conventions were attracted to Portland, and brought together members (among others) of the National Conference of Charities and Corrections, the Order of Railway Conductors and the American Association of Traveling Passenger Agents. The National Good Roads Association met at the same time that the transcontinental Olds pulled into Portland, but that association unfortunately left a $1,440 stack of unpaid bills. On August 16 through 19, the Trans-Mississippi Commercial Congress reaffirmed the booster function of the Exposition. Local arrangements were in the hands of the Portland Chamber of Commerce and the Commercial Club, whose executive committee overlapped the Exposition Board (Theodore Wilcox, A.L. Mills, J.C. Ainsworth, I.N. Fleischner) and whose manager, Tom Richardson, showered welcome and unwelcome advice on Henry Goode throughout the summer. Keynoters at the sessions in the Festival Hall and Chapman School included David Parry of the National Association of Manufacturers, former Secretary of the Interior David Francis, and the head of the newly named U.S. Forest Service, Gifford Pinchot.

Standard admission to the extravaganza was 50¢ for adults and 25¢ for children, with additional charges to watch the diving elk or the warbling Venetians. If a regular visitor was willing to sit for a mug shot with a number hung around his neck, he could purchase a non-transferable ticket book—137 tickets for $20.00 or 50 tickets for $12.50. After the first weeks of June, when cold nights and damp days left restaurants empty and exhibit halls echoing, John Wakefield added a book of 25 tickets at $7.50 for family use. Despite the filigree of electric lights that outlined the bridges, balustrades and buildings, less than twenty percent of the visitors entered after 6:00

P.M. As a special premium, the company offered 25¢ in free coupons for The Trail with each evening full-price admission.

Daily paid attendance averaged 11,600. Special programs boosted the gate on "state days"; the Fourth of July celebrations attracted over 50,000. On September 30, the Exposition went all out for Portland Day, when out-of-town fairgoers were down to a trickle. Mayor Harry Lane officially proclaimed that the honor and good name of the city required a turnout of 100,000. To pad the count, Henry Goode asked all the Exposition workers to sacrifice use of free passes and to pay at least one admission. Beachey's aeronautic voyage that day was a publicity stunt; he delivered a message about Portland Day to downtown businessmen. The actual crowd of 85,149 braved a chilly drizzle for special concerts by Ellery's Royal Italians and DeCaprio's Administration Band, a boomerang exhibition, another flight by the *City of Portland*, and a miniature version of the Battle of Manila Bay.

Although Portland Day fell short of the attendance goal, total attendance at the Exposition more than matched expectations. In 1904, Jefferson Myers had predicted 1,000,000 visitors and the *Oregonian* had raised his projection to 1,370,000 in January, 1905. From June 1 through the official closing on October 15, the gatekeepers in fact counted 1,588,000 paid admissions. Free passes to reporters, workmen, officials and others accounted for another 966,000 visits. The editorial writer who, in 1904, had argued that the Fair's attendance would depend on "our own people" from the Pacific states was correct. The attendance records show that thirty-four percent came from Portland, forty percent from elsewhere in Oregon and Washington, sixteen percent from California and the mountain states, and ten percent from east of the Rockies.

Hundreds of thousands of visitors created special problems of law and order. Early in the summer, the Exposition's "Secret Service" cracked a ring of gatekeepers and ticket sellers who had skimmed $5,000 off the receipts. One company agent worked in each building as a janitor, to watch for petty thievery from exhibits or patrons. The city council also passed an ordinance outlawing the scalping of railroad excursion tickets and deputized a special railroad detective. Swindlers and bunco artists were a special worry. The Portland Police and the Exposition's Secret Service compiled 2,000 pictures of notorious pickpockets and confidence men, and checked strange faces against the file. Prison wardens in the western states passed the word at the release of dangerous convicts. The return from the effort seems modest; fifty-five known criminals were apprehended and ejected from the grounds.

Protection of tourists outside the Exposition was a different story. Portland could not match Seattle's boomtown vices, but it had its share of pleasures for the sophisticated and snares for the unwary. The *Portland Telegram* was particularly concerned about the Arnold Brothers dance hall, which stood ready near the Fair to entice wayward youths on their way home from the fisheries exhibit or the Vaughn Street baseball park. The shadiest side of Portland nestled near the waterfront and the railroad station. There were opium dens on the fringes of Chinatown, streetwalkers to meet the trains, and saloons where it was simple to follow drink with debauchery. The whole district flourished under the eye of "special police," who wore city uniforms and badges but who drew their pay from private businessmen.

Portland architect Edgar M. Lazarus designed the Palace of Agriculture, a building that occupied an area of 200x450 feet. In an official souvenir book its contents were described: "Within the walls a most wonderful display of fruits of the earth is seen. . . . Fanciful shapes, formed from cereals, show wonderful cunning and ingenuity." Frederic Remington's statue, "Hitting the Trail," can be seen behind the promenaders.

Rising in the middle of the lake the United States Government Building (ABOVE) lured visitors to its gleaming towers and classical colonnades from the moment they entered the Exposition gates. Located in the main building (among other exhibits) were displays of the departments of War, Treasury and Post Office, and the bureaus of Agriculture and Mining. Auxiliary buildings on each side housed the Fish Commission and the Alaska and Philippines exhibits.

The "Timber Temple," (ABOVE RIGHT) Oregon's charmingly anomalous Forestry Building, rose conspicuously on the southwest edge of the Exposition's central cluster. In contrast to the white façades of its neighbors, this 100x200-foot structure was constructed completely of unhewn logs, many weighing over 32 tons and measuring as much as 6 feet across and 60 feet long.

Behind the Aeronautic Concourse and overlooking Guild's Lake, the American Inn (BELOW RIGHT) stood apart from the main exposition area. With 585 rooms it provided about 10 percent of the city's total public accommodations for overnight guests.

At the turn of the century, with air travel still largely a curiosity, balloonists successfully rivaled most other stuntmen at fairs. During the Exposition a number of flights originated at the Aeronautic Concourse (the open area beyond the fence in the foreground) behind The Trail, which drew large crowds during take-off and landing times.

Located several miles from the heart of downtown Portland, for many fairgoers access to the Exposition grounds required public transportation. The city's trolley cars generally proved the best mode of travel. Without them, to be sure, Portland would have been ill-equipped to handle its one million visitors, who, arriving from all areas of the country, found overnight quarters in many different parts of the host city.

This daytime view of the Great Extravaganza corresponds to the night picture opposite. The photographer, who stood above Lakeview Avenue facing north to take this shot, included (from the foreground) the Grand Stairway, the Grand Bandstand, the Esplanade, part of The Trail, the Bridge of Nations and the U.S. Government Building. On the far shores of Guild's Lake, industrial establishments can be seen; for visitors in the gleaming fairgrounds, however, their presence did not intrude upon the fairy-tale quality of the Exposition.

The *Oregon Journal* Souvenir Book describes this vivid scene: "Night works a transformation at the Fair. Every graceful line and curve is softened, every mass of color subdued, everything is under the witchery of the effulgence produced by uncounted lights. The scene is beautiful by day, but at night it is another picture and an entrancing one. The lights steal gently forth, first with a dull glow, then more boldly, until at last every great building, and statue, and bridge, is outlined and festooned with countless glowing points that combine to shed radiance over all."

Souvenir ticket issued September 30, 1905, designated Portland Day at the Lewis and Clark Exposition. The festivities were devised as much to honor the Great Extravaganza's promoters and backers as to commemorate the anniversary of its host city's incorporation. The daily program (see p. 66), handed out with each admission, indicates the dual nature of the celebration; it contained the following tribute by president of the Exposition H.W. Goode: "Today the Imperial Rose City fetes herself and celebrates the success of the Centennial Exposition. . . . The record of Portland Day shall stand for many years as a testimonial to the public spirit and enterprise of the business men of this city. Their money and their time were heavily pledged in this undertaking."

IV

The Balance Sheet

It is impossible to check the books of the bars and bawdy houses after three-quarters of a century, but we can assess the overall impact of the Lewis and Clark Fair on the Portland economy. The Exposition Company surprised even its backers by showing an operating profit. Its receipts from 1902 through 1905 amounted to $1,524,655: $405,085 from subscriptions to its capital stock, $735,007 from admissions, $51,428 from the sale of souvenir gold coins, $247,528 from concessions and $85,607 from salvage and miscellaneous sources. The cost of organization and construction was $918,560 and the cost of operations and wind-up was $521,634. When the corporation's business was finished in early 1906, the cash-on-hand difference between receipts and expenditures was $84,461.

The question of profits brought yet another conflict between the corporation and the state commission. Jefferson Myers claimed a share of the remaining funds for the state, arguing that the money rightfully belonged to the people of Oregon. The Exposition's board of directors, however, believed that the Fair had been a private enterprise and the $84,461 was private property to be distributed as a twenty-one percent return of the original capital invested. The dispute went to Attorney General A.W. Crawford, who mulled the issue over the New Year's holiday and returned his opinion on January 2, 1906. He found no evidence that the legislature had intended joint business management or the mixing of state and corporate funds. The state commission had been forbidden to take on additional obligations beyond those explicitly authorized, and Myers had scrupulously avoided overstepping the legislative limits. Since the state through the commission could not share deficits with the company, Crawford concluded, it could scarcely expect to share surpluses.

Most of the Fair's ancillary enterprises failed to match even the moderate success of the corporation. The Division of Exploitation was forced to subsidize the *Lewis and Clark Journal* after its first few issues, and terminated it in July as a painful drain on company cash. Exposition directors who hoped to make money on the side with the American Inn ended up losing most of their investment. Portland businessmen who backed the attractions of The Trail found that construction and operating costs exceeded their intake. Though visitors had to pass along The Trail to reach the federal buildings, they apparently saved their money for 10¢ vaudeville shows downtown or unmentioned pleasures in Chinatown. The elaborate Carnival of Venice, for one example, would have closed its doors and beached its gondolas without the quiet assistance from the Exposition management.

The real economic benefits resulted from spending outside the Exposition grounds. The Fair attracted 540,000 visitors from Portland, 640,000 from elsewhere in Oregon and Washington, and 408,000 from the rest of the United States and Canada. We can estimate that the Exposition drew approximately 800,000 customers for Portland hotels, where cheap rooms went for 50¢ and expensive for $5.00. If each visitor stayed three days and two nights, he or she probably spent $4.50 on food and drink, $3.00 on lodging, and another $2.50 on porters, postcards, souvenirs, theatres and trolleys. This would have infused around $8,000,000 into the stream of Portland commerce. For comparison, Portland's workshops and factories paid roughly $7,000,000

Exposition promoters did their best to encourage and facilitate repeat attendance. One tactic was the season pass; an-

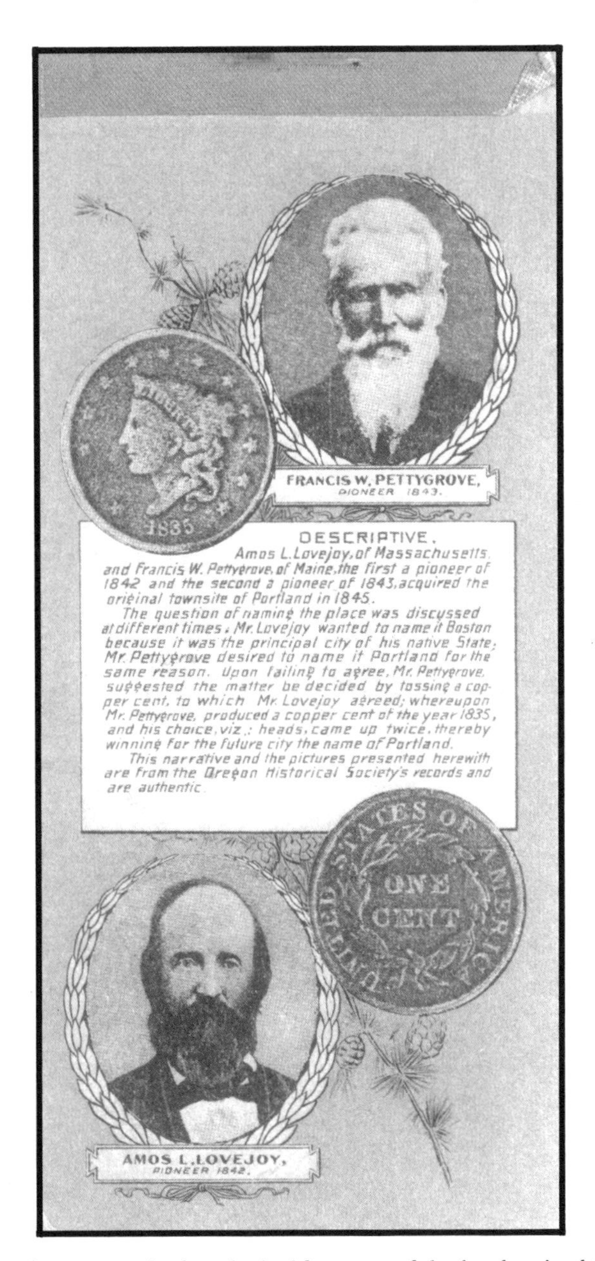

other was the ticket book, whose purchase price depended on the number of coupons inside. The purchaser's photograph was attached to the inside cover of the book—in this case, 50 separate visits could be enjoyed.

Daily Official Program

WORLD'S FAIR PORTLAND.

Published by Albert Hess & Co. *Price, 10c* *Printed by Bushong & Co.*

NUMBER 122 SATURDAY SEPTEMBER 30

PORTLAND DAY

GRAND PARADE
TWO AIRSHIP FLIGHTS
DRESS PARADE OF U. S. REGULAR TROOPS
THE ELLARY ROYAL ITALIAN BAND
GRAND DISPLAY FIREWORKS
BOOMERANG EXHIBITION
JAPANESE DAY FIREWORKS
ASSOCIATION FOOTBALL
BATTLE OF MINILLA

ORDER OF THE DAY.

7:00 a. m. Gates open.
7:00 a. m. Municipal salute.
9:00 a. m. Concert, Administration Band, Transportation building.
10:00 a. m. Concert, Administration Band, Gray boulevard.
11:00 a. m. Airship flight.
12:00 m. State salute.
12:00 m. Dress parade.
1:00 p. m. Airship flight.
2:00 p. m. Boomerang exhibition.
2:00 p. m. Organ recital, F. W. Goodrich, Forestry building.
2:30 p. m. Concert, the Ellery Royal Italian Band, Gray boulevard.
2:30 p. m. Life-saving exhibition.
3:00 p. m. Grand parade
4:00 p. m. Japanese fireworks.
6:00 p. m. National salute.
8:00 p. m. Fireworks.
8:20 p. m. Battle of Manila.
9:00 p. m. Concert, the Ellery Royal Italian Band, Gray boulevard.
10:30 p. m. Distribution of prizes.
11:30 p. m. Trail closes.
12:00 p. m. Grounds dark.
See special events.

Don't miss the famous Portland Heights loop ride.

Special Bargains in O cial Souvenir Spoons at all spoon booths on the grounds.

Don't fail to visit the **Singer Sewing Machine exhibit in Manufacturers' Building.**

Issued daily, the Exposition's official program included a map, schedule, advertisements and other promotional information on the Fair and its host city. This cover and schedule appeared on Portland Day, which opened at 7:00 AM with a municipal 55-gun salute to commemorate the 55th anniversary of Portland's incorporation. Two more special salutes (state and national), special concerts, an airship flight, fireworks, a boomerang-throwing exhibition, mock naval battle and cash prizes totaling $1,000 carried the official celebration to 10:30 PM; an exhausted but exultant staff—this had been the peak attendance day—closed the Exposition gates at midnight.

This view of the Exposition's main entrance (located at what is now 26th and Upshur) was photographed on Portland Day. Hoping for a banner turnout for the city's anniversary festivities, promoters advertised September 30 by equating attendance with loyalty to Portland. To capitalize on potentially large profits, free passes were voided and all visitors and workers were required to pay full price for entry. The attendance goal was achieved as a record 85,149 visitors passed through the gates. Thus, triumphantly noted by follow-up coverage, Portland outdid the best day of Omaha's 1898 Trans-Mississippi Exposition by more than 25,000 admissions.

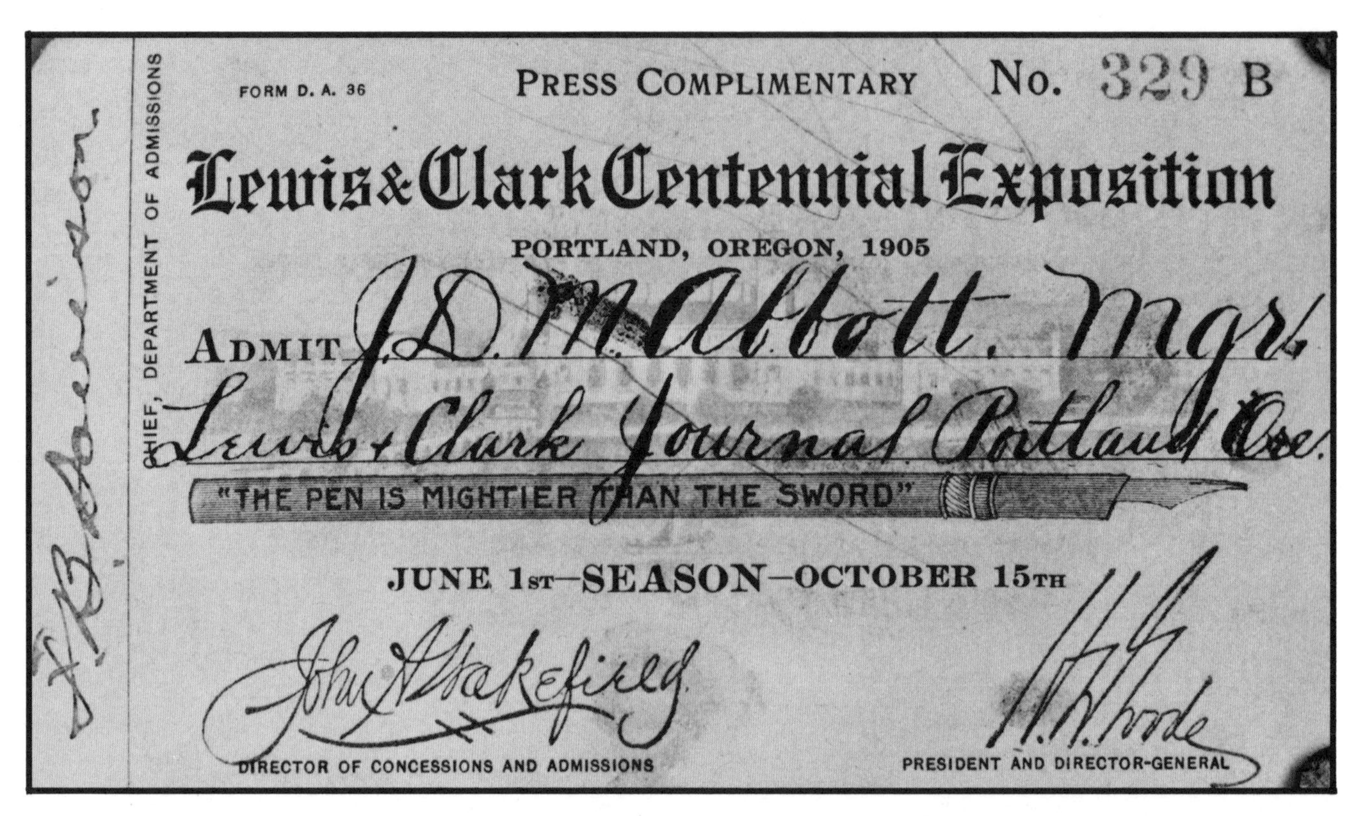
FORM D. A. 36

PRESS COMPLIMENTARY No. 329 B

Lewis & Clark Centennial Exposition

PORTLAND, OREGON, 1905

ADMIT J. D. M. Abbott, Mgr.
Lewis + Clark Journal Portland Ore.

"THE PEN IS MIGHTIER THAN THE SWORD"

JUNE 1ST—SEASON—OCTOBER 15TH

DIRECTOR OF CONCESSIONS AND ADMISSIONS

PRESIDENT AND DIRECTOR-GENERAL

CHIEF, DEPARTMENT OF ADMISSIONS

For widespread influence on potential attendance, the press could hardly be ignored, so the Exposition courted favorable attention by providing members of the fourth estate free tickets to the festivities. In the case of this press pass holder, however, a negative response would have been unlikely. The *Lewis and Clark Journal* was founded independently in 1904 to convey, through its focus on the history and character of the Northwest, the sectional and national character of the Exposition; later that year, due to declining subscriptions, the *Journal* was taken over by the Corporation, whose editor continued to stress the Fair's progress and Portland's attractions in the monthly issues.

in salaries and wages to their 9,000 employees in 1905. In 1980, convention bureau economists assume that 400 visitor-days support one tourist-industry job. By the same standard, Portland's summer guests would have created 5,000 extra jobs for the duration of the Fair, in a city whose total work force was 65,000.

The Exposition's construction budget also affected Portland's balance sheet. Expenditures on buildings and grounds totaled $300,000 for the state commission, $250,000 for the United States government, and $538,000 for the corporation. Smaller buildings erected by participating states and corporations and new hotels outside the grounds raised the total above $1,300,000. Again, by comparison, the annual value of building permits in the city averaged $4,000,000 in 1903, 1904 and 1905, and employment in the building trades was approximately 4,000. From the spring of 1904 through the spring of 1905, it seems safe to suggest that the Exposition provided an extra 1,000 construction jobs.

The question of economic impacts and profits raises the broader issue of private gain and public benefit. The possibility of conflicting interests has become more bothersome in our self-conscious times than it was in the confident years of the Exposition. The Fair was a community enterprise shared by the city and the state. It received support from the legislature, enthusiastic participation by local school boards and county commissions, and full assistance from two very different city administrations. It also enjoyed the backing and participation of Portland's civic and business elite, who made no clear distinction between public and private responsibilities for promoting their city's growth. In organizing the Lewis and Clark Exposition, these citizens believed that they were working with popular approval for the public good. If the rich got richer with the Exposition, it was not because of dubious deals but because their economic interests were identified with the city. They gained profit from anything that stimulated urban growth—including the Exposition—because their real estate holdings, bank partnerships, downtown businesses, suburban subdivisions, and streetcar stock all amounted to speculations in the future of Portland.

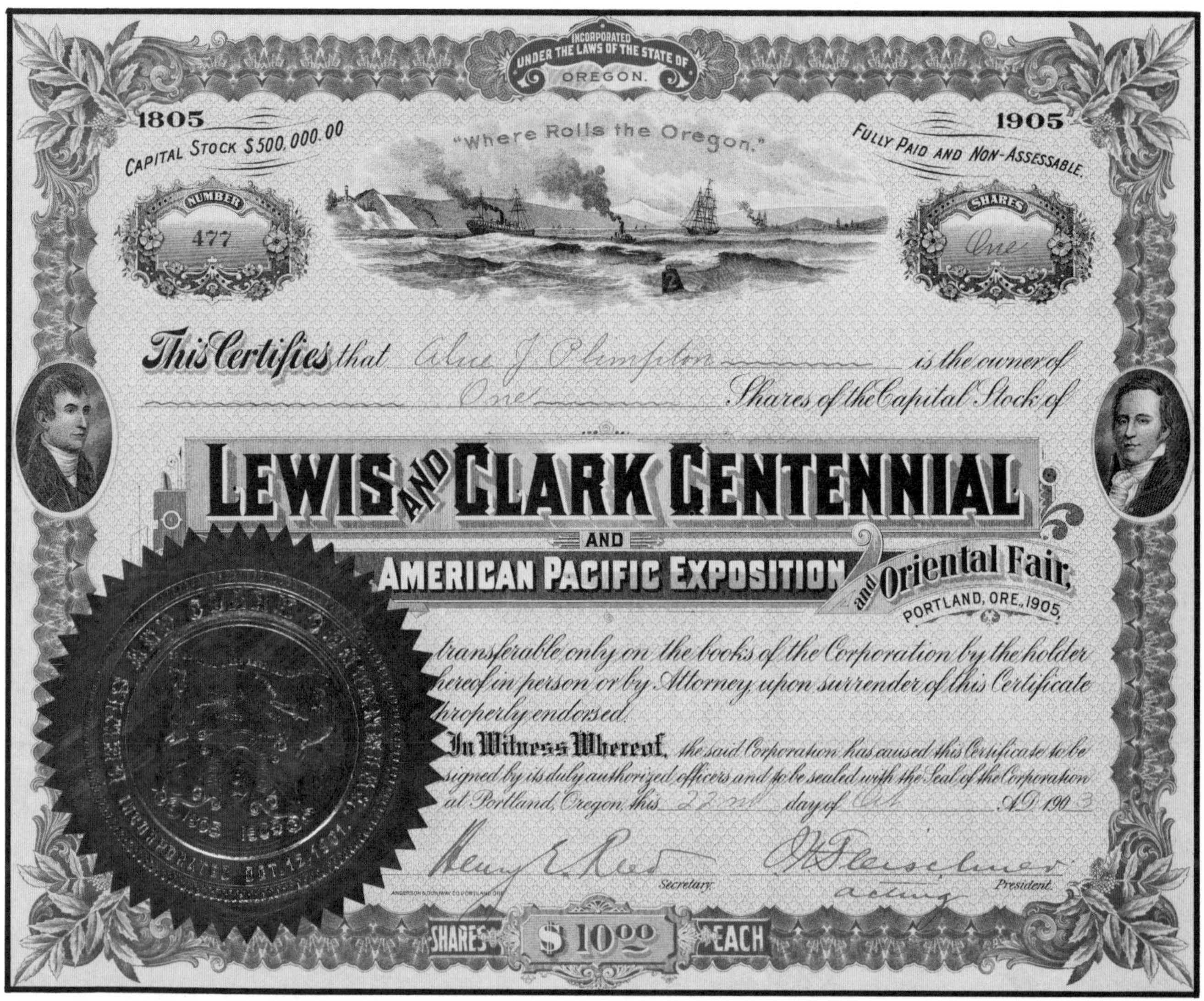
INCORPORATED UNDER THE LAWS OF THE STATE OF OREGON.

1805 1905

CAPITAL STOCK $500,000.00

FULLY PAID AND NON-ASSESSABLE.

"Where Rolls the Oregon."

NUMBER 477

SHARES One

This Certifies that Alice J Plimpton is the owner of One Shares of the Capital Stock of

LEWIS AND CLARK CENTENNIAL AND AMERICAN PACIFIC EXPOSITION and Oriental Fair, PORTLAND, ORE., 1905,

transferable only on the books of the Corporation by the holder hereof in person or by Attorney upon surrender of this Certificate properly endorsed.

In Witness Whereof, the said Corporation has caused this Certificate to be signed by its duly authorized officers and to be sealed with the Seal of the Corporation at Portland, Oregon, this 22nd day of Oct A.D. 1903

Henry E. Reed, Secretary.

acting President.

SHARES $10.00 EACH

This stock certificate was issued in October 1903, during one of a number of Lewis and Clark Centennial stock sales; the earliest sale took place in late November 1902. Alice Plimpton's single share is indicative of the broad financial support given to the Fair by governments, businesses and private persons.

V

The Exposition and the City

The balance sheets for the Exposition Company and for Portland were gratifying, but the key to overall success was the impression that Portland and its extravaganza made on visiting journalists and investors. A favorable reception was not a foregone conclusion, for only two years later the national press was to savage the city of Norfolk, Virginia, and its Jamestown Fair for all the problems that Portland had worked so hard to avoid, from price gouging to poor transportation to unfinished buildings. *Leslie's Weekly* described "the latest great exposition" as "Portland's pride." "The whole fair," said *The World's Work*, "is a successful effort to express . . . the natural richness of the country and its relative nearness to Asia." Walter Hines Page, editor of *The World's Work*, summarized the consensus when he told eastern readers that "the enterprise has from the beginning been managed with modesty, good sense, and good taste."

The first notices in Portland were just as glowing. The *Oregonian* and the *Pacific Monthly* both marked the Exposition's closing day with editorial tributes to Portland enthusiasm and regional cooperation. Portlanders agreed that the city could take permanent pride in a Fair that had surpassed every expectation. A year's reflection did nothing to change the belief that "the Lewis and Clark Exposition was a great thing for Oregon." *Oregonian* reporters interviewed George Chamberlain, H.W. Goode, Tom Richardson, Wallis Nash of the Board of Trade, and other leading citizens in October, 1906. To a man, they shared the newspaper's editorial opinion that "the Lewis and Clark Exposition officially marked the end of the old and the beginning of the new Oregon." Portland and its sister cities of the Northwest, said Richardson, had "caught step in the great march of progress."

The "great march" was in fact the onset of the greatest economic boom that Portland has ever experienced. The first indirect impact of the Fair was a shortage of office space during the magnificent summer itself. By the end of the Exposition, real estate dealers had counted the investment of $800,000 in new business buildings and plans for $1,000,000 more. Portland department store owners Julius Meier, Adolphe Wolfe, and H.C. Wortman all reported impressive growth of retail sales early in 1906. Outside purchases of Portland land and buildings triggered a flow of funds from previously cautious Portlanders, and real estate values advanced between twenty-five and fifty percent during the course of 1906. The same year work commenced on the North Bank Railroad along the Columbia from Pasco to Portland, Swift and Company's huge new packing plant in north Portland, and eastern capital was invested in the newly consolidated Portland Railway Light and Power Company.

From 1905 through 1911, every economic indicator reflected extraordinary prosperity. Bank clearings increased by 150 percent. The value of building permits jumped by 458 percent, from $4,183,000 in 1905 to $20,886,000 in 1910 and $19,152,000 in 1911. One result of the building boom was the construction of Portland's third business district. In the 1870s and 1880s, the original wooden buildings of "Stumptown" had given way to three- and four-story business blocks. Now, the new surge of growth required massive new office space to meet the city's expanded business, with skyscrapers of ten or twelve or fourteen floors on Fifth and Sixth and new office complexes of five and six stories from Third to Broadway. There were new buildings for Meier and Frank Co., Lipman, Wolfe and Co., a new public library, and the new Oregon Hotel (later the Benson). The new city was brighter as well as taller, built with light brick and glazed terra cotta rather than the heavy stone and dark red brick of the nineteenth century.

Portland also built a new middle-class city on the east side of the Willamette. Homes and homeowners followed trolley lines north to Woodlawn and University Park, east beyond the city limits to Rose City Park, Mount Tabor, and Woodstock. Streetcar traffic doubled and doubled again as Portland added 2,400 houses and apartments each year during the Exposition boom. Between 1900 and 1916, the old westside neighborhoods grew from 58,000 to 96,000 residents by packing families more tightly into already developed areas. Over the same period the east side grew from 32,000 to 178,000 and remained more populated than the west side for two generations. To serve the new neighborhoods, Portland replaced the old Morrison, Hawthorne and Steel bridges between 1905 and 1912 and opened a new Broadway bridge in 1913. In 1910, at the height of the boom, Building Inspector H.E. Plummer reported 132 new houses west of the river and 3,000 east.

As the boom peaked and began to fade in 1912 and 1913, Portlanders sat back to evaluate their good fortune. Community leaders took it for granted that the Fair had been the key to their seven years of extraordinary economic growth. "It seems that confidence came with the Exposition," wrote C.H. Williams of the Commercial Club in *Bankers Magazine*. Former U.S. Vice-President Charles Fairbanks marveled over the skyscrapers new since his visit in 1905 and told a reporter from the *Telegram* that "no place that I know of has made such remarkable development and progress." "Its entry into the really big city class is a matter of the past half decade," said another local business leader. Portland historian Joseph Gaston, in his *Portland, Oregon: Its History and Builders*, summed up the consensus in 1911:

> *The very decision to hold the exposition, strengthened every man that put down a dollar for it; and from that very day Portland business, Portland real estate, and Portland's great future commenced to move up—to move with confidence, courage, steadfastness, and accelerating energy; and the movement never halted or hesitated from that day to this. The exposition . . . attracted hundreds of thousands of people, many of them wealthy, to this city, who knew nothing of the advantages of Portland and its surroundings. They were surprised and pleased at what they found and learned, and went away to spread the story of Portland's beauty and future prospects, and then came back to invest their money in Portland property and business.*

Ironically the Exposition boom had lesser impact on northwest Portland than on the east side. The location and topography of the Guild's Lake site, which had made it suitable for a fairgrounds, limited its subsequent use. John Olmsted's city-wide plan of 1903 had proposed the conversion of the site to public open space, with a strip of parkland linking Macleay Park to the river across the heart of the exhibition area and a riverfront park covering the peninsula and northern end of the lake. Within a week of the close of the Fair, however, the *Oregonian* was arguing that a park at Guild's Lake would violate Olmsted's own principles. The Fair site, said the paper, was too large for a playground, too isolated for a neighborhood park, and too expensive in comparison with suburban land in the West Hills or along the Columbia. The *Oregonian*'s assessment was confirmed during 1906, when Seattle and eastern investors, operating through the Portland Development Company, spent $500,000 to buy the various land parcels. Portland voters approved a $1,000,000 bond issue for parks in 1907, but the money did not become available until 1909 and 1910. With land price inflation, that allocation was consumed by the purchase of Sellwood, Peninsula, Laurelhurst and Mount Tabor parks and the start of work on Terwilliger Boulevard.

The Guild's Lake site was largely cleared by the time the Portland Development Company closed its deals. The construction agreement between the corporation and state commission required removal of the major buildings by March 1, 1906. The only exception was the Forestry Building. A special act of the legislature required the commission to donate this building to the city if Portland purchased its site, as in fact the city council agreed to do. A few of the smaller buildings were moved to new locations—the Massachusetts Building to Mount Tabor for use as a sanitarium, the Masonic Building to 26th and Northrup, the National Cash Register Building to Ivanhoe and Richmond in north Portland. A few other buildings on the edges of the site remained in use for several years. As late as 1908 the second floor of the Administration Building, adjacent to the main entrance, was a dwelling. The nearby Administration Restaurant became a metalworks school, and the elegant Oregon Building a kindergarten. The Illinois Building remained as rental property near the carriage entrance on Nicolai. The Oriental Exhibits Building also remained standing until 1911.

When Edward H. Bennett prepared his comprehensive plan for a "Greater Portland" in 1910-11, the flat lands of northwest Portland seemed appropriate only for industrial development. Bennett expected the central business district to spread north and west from the railroad terminal along a new diagonal avenue to be cut from Park and Burnside to Twenty-Third and Thurman. He also proposed to deepen the natural channel of the Willamette between Swan Island and Mock's Bottom, connect Swan Island and the southeast end of the Exposition site with landfill, and line the new cul-de-sac with slips and dock facilities cut into Guild's Lake and into the southwest side of Swan Island.

Guild's Lake itself disappeared under a deluge of silt between 1910 and 1913. After a false and illegal start by speculator Lafe Pence in 1907, the Lewis-Wiley Company of Seattle constructed a system of high pressure hoses and flumes to carve the streets and lots of Westover Terrace out of the West Hills and sluice the suspended dirt into the shallow lake. Wooden forms were used to shape the terraces, and by the middle of the decade the first houses speckled the hillside. The new landfill that covered the old lake took longer to settle. Except for the construction of Montgomery Ward in 1921 and a scattering of other industrial buildings on the higher ground, the old fairgrounds and new mud flats remained largely unoccupied during the next two decades of slow growth in Portland. Indeed, as late as 1942 and 1943 the western half of the site was immediately available for 2,600 units of emergency war housing.

Portland staged the Lewis and Clark Exposition to declare its entry into the new century. In the short term, the Fair initiated a golden age of prosperity. The $10,000,000 spent by sponsors, participants, and visitors multiplied and remultiplied its impact on demand for services and facilities. As late as 1904, Portlanders had felt daring to predict a population of 200,000. By 1911 and 1912, they thought it reasonable to project targets yet to be reached—as high as four million. The Fair also symbolized Portland's willingness to accept the men and measures required by a new era. The excuse may have been commemoration of a historic event, but the theme was the potential of commerce with the rim of the Pacific. The motif was the pleasures and possibilities of twentieth-century technology—airships and automobiles, incubators and electricity.

The Exposition confirmed a new generation of civic leaders. Portland was fifty years old when planning started and fifty-four when the Fair was celebrated. It had been dominated in the 1870s, 1880s, and 1890s by the businessmen who had followed the first settlers, picked up the pieces from early failures, and built careers in tandem with the growing city. By 1903, however, journalist Ray Stannard Baker noted that "the sons of the pioneers are now coming into power." The transition could be seen in the Exposition Company, whose first two presidents represented the old era. Henry Corbett led the company's organization and headed its operations until his death in 1903 at the age of seventy-six. Harvey Scott was in his mid-sixties during his term as president in 1903-04, and died in 1910. Their successor, H.W. Goode, was forty-two during the Exposition year. He was neither a journalist like Scott nor a universal entrepreneur like Corbett, but rather the new-style American professional business executive, with a career in the growing electric power industry. A.H. Devers followed work

On June 30, 1930, a local aerial survey firm took this photograph of the former site of the Lewis and Clark Exposition—little remained of the Great Extravaganza. The Portland-Astoria Road can be seen curving into the city through the western boundary of the old Exposition grounds. Just to the left of the curve stands the large, white structure of the Montgomery Ward store, sitting astride the former position of the Sunken Gardens. Barely discernible to the right of the Wards building is the roof of the Forestry Building, which would stand until it was destroyed by fire in the 1960s. Today, the large open area is filled with both heavy industry and railroad-oriented firms.

on the Exposition board by serving as head of the Manufacturers Association and helping to organize the Civic Improvement League that brought Edward Bennett to Portland. J.C. Ainsworth worked on the Exposition, invested his money in the telephone industry, pushed for park bonds, joined the Civic Improvement League, and served on the first planning commission in 1919. In all, the Exposition provided a graceful transition of civic responsibility between two like-minded generations of businessmen.

The Lewis and Clark Exposition can be summed up simply. It was a community enterprise in an age of confidence.

Portland's ability to stage an extravaganza without the nagging problems that injured other expositions promised even greater success for the future. In the 1970s and for the 1980s, the key words in political discussions have become "trade-offs," "limits," and "conservation." For a brief moment seventy-five years ago, the Exposition suggested something very different. The formal elegance and order of the Exposition grounds and buildings reflected a society that was remarkably unified and stable for a city only a few years and a few miles removed from the logging frontier. The electric lights outlining the exhibition halls and the Bridge of Nations illuminated the path to a prosperous future. The green hills, brown river, and white mountains were a reminder of the continued pleasures of Portland's setting. The elements of the panorama taken together seemed to promise Portlanders the best of all worlds, a city and a century without limits.

Sources

A convenient starting point for information on the origins and progress of the Lewis and Clark Exposition is the editorials and news columns of Portland's daily newspapers, especially the *Oregonian* and the *Telegram*. Another is the unpublished history by Exposition executive Henry Reed, available at the Oregon History Center.

For more information on decisions behind the Fair, the central office correspondence of the Exposition Company at the Oregon History Center fills the equivalent of half-a-dozen file cabinets. The Oregon State Archives has records of the state commission dealing with the St. Louis Fair and with construction at Guild's Lake. The Mayor's office correspondence at the Portland City Archives is another useful source. The public views of the Exposition and the city can be found in the locally edited *Pacific Monthly* and *Lewis and Clark Journal*, in the record of hearings before the House of Representatives Committee on Industrial Arts and Expositions, and in articles in such national magazines as *Harper's Weekly*, *World's Work*, *Review of Reviews*, *Bankers Magazine*, *The Century*, and *Architectural Record*. Official publications include the catalog of exhibits, guide books, daily programs and the report of the state commission. Contemporary maps, photographs, and city directories are all essential sources for reconstructing the physical appearance of Portland during and after the Fair.

Other recent evaluations of the Exposition and its impacts can be found in Robert W. Rydell, *All the World's a Fair: Visions of Empire at American International Expositions, 1876–1916*, (Chicago: University of Chicago Press, 1984) and Holly J. Pruitt, *A "Sense of Place . . . Pride . . . and Identity:" Portland's 1905 Lewis and Clark Fair* (B.A. thesis, Reed College, 1985). Portland and its Exposition in 1905 provide the setting for Joel Redon's novel *If Not on Earth, Then in Heaven* (New York: St. Martin's Press, 1991).

INDEX

Italicized numbers indicate illustrations and captions

About the Author

Carl Abbott is Professor of Urban Studies and Planning at Portland State University, where he has taught since 1978. He is the author of an number of books on the history of American cities and planning in the Pacific Northwest, including the *Metropolitan Frontier: Cities in the Modern American West* (1993). He received his graduate degrees from the University of Chicago, adjacent to the site of the World's Columbian Exposition of 1893.

Colophon

The Great Extravaganza was typeset in Janson, a typeface incorrectly attributed to Anton Janson (1620–1687), a Dutch typefounder who resided mostly in Leipzig. The original version of this face was designed by the Hungarian Miklós Kis (pronounced keesh) in 1690. The face is noted for its unusual capital M and the ear on the lowercase g. Janson is a classic Humanist face, part of a group referred to as Old Style. It has been a favorite of book designers for three centuries.

This volume is printed in 80 lb. Strathmore Grande natural and bound in 12 pt. Springhill. The typesetting was done by Irish Setter of Portland, Oregon, and the printing by Paramount Graphics of Beaverton, Oregon.

The Great Extravaganza was edited and designed by Bruce Taylor Hamilton, with the assistance of Tracy Ann Robinson and Colleen Campbell.